SPEAKING OF BODIES

SPEAKING OF BODIES

Embodied Therapeutic Dialogues

Edited by

Asaf Rolef Ben-Shahar, Liron Lipkies, and Noa Oster

Routledge
Taylor & Francis Group

LONDON AND NEW YORK

First published 2016 by
Karnac Books Ltd.

Published 2018 by Routledge
2 Park Square, Milton Park, Abingdon, Oxon OX14 4RN
711 Third Avenue, New York, NY 10017, USA

Routledge is an imprint of the Taylor & Francis Group, an informa business

British Library Cataloguing in Publication Data

A C.I.P. for this book is available from the British Library

ISBN 9781782202042 (pbk)

Edited, designed and produced by The Studio Publishing Services Ltd
www.publishingservicesuk.co.uk
e-mail: studio@publishingservicesuk.co.uk

CONTENTS

PART II
THE LIVING BODY

PART III
THE SENSUAL BODY

PART IV
THE BODY OF PAIN

Janet Balaskas was born in South Africa and moved to London in the 1960s. She is a leading author and pioneer in the field of childbirth, in particular the reclaiming of the power of birth by women. She coined the phrase "Active Birth" in the 1980s to describe a birth in which a woman is actively in charge of her body, choices, and decisions. She founded the Active Birth Centre in London where she teaches both parents and professionals, and also works extensively internationally.

John Conger, PhD, is a psychologist and psychoanalyst, and also an international trainer in Bioenergetic Analysis. He is the author of *Jung and Reich: the Body as Shadow* (1988) and *The Body in Recovery: Somatic Psychotherapy and the Self* (1994). Dr Conger teaches at Meridian University, and conducts his own training in analytic and somatic practice. He has a private practice in Berkeley, California.

Michael Eigen, PhD, teaches and practises in New York City. He has given private seminars on Bion, Winnicott, and his own work for over forty years, and has an online Yahoo group. He has published twenty-four books and many papers. He is an associate professor of clinical psychology (adjunct) at New York University Postdoctoral Program in

Psychotherapy and Psychoanalysis, and a senior faculty member and training/control analyst at the National Psychological Association for Psychoanalysis.

Ohad Ezrahi is a lead faculty in ISTA—the International School of Temple Arts (www.schooloftemplearts.org) that teaches Sexual Shamanism around the world. He is also the founder and spiritual director of Neviah—the Hebraic Academy of Universal Spirit, based in Tel Aviv. Ohad was ordained as a Rabbi in 1999 by Rabbi Zalman Schakter-Shalomi and as a Zen Dharma Holder by Roshi Berney Glassman in 2011. He created the cards system of "The BresLove Cards" and is the author of six books in Neo-Kabbalistic thought, including *Who's afraid of Lilith* (Hebrew). Ohad is an artist and a musician, his first album, *Something out of Chaos*, was released in 2012. Together with his wife Dawn Cherie he created the teachings of Kabalove© and The School of Love in Kabala. They teach and lead workshops in Israel, Europe, and America.

Steven H. Knoblauch, PhD, is faculty and supervisor at The New York University Postdoctoral Program in Psychotherapy and Psychoanalysis, The Institute for the Psychoanalytic Study of Subjectivity, the Institute for Contemporary Psychotherapy, and the Psychoanalytic Psychology Study Center, all in New York City. He is also faculty at the Stephen A. Mitchell Center for Relational Studies. He is author of *The Musical Edge of Therapeutic Dialogue* (2000, Analytic Press) and co-author with Beatrice Beebe, Dorienne Sorter, and Judith Rustin of *Forms of Intersubjectivity in Infant Research and Adult Treatment* (2005, Other Press).

Yasmin Levy is an internationally acclaimed Israeli Ladino and Spanish singer. Born and still living in Jerusalem, she is the daughter of Isaac Levy, the respected Spanish and Ladino musicologist who documented much of the Ladino canon. Her debut album *Romance & Yasmin* was released in 2000, and she was nominated for the 2005 BBC world music award. Since then she has released five more albums. Yasmin Levy was honoured with the EU's Anna Lindh Award for cross-cultural collaboration and also won the USA Songwriting Competition in the world music category for her song *Me Voy*. www.yasminlevy.net

Liron Lipkies is a relational body psychotherapist, accredited by the European Association of Body Psychotherapy, and a yoga therapist. She is part of the teaching faculty at Psychosoma, the post graduate body psychotherapy school at the Israeli Centre for Body Mind Medicine. Liron finds nature an inspiring teacher for working with people, for living life, and as a ground for being in relationships.

Noa Oster is a relational body psychotherapist, accredited by the European Association of Body Psychotherapy. She lectures and teaches at Psychosoma, the post graduate relational body psychotherapy school at the Israeli Centre for Body Mind Medicine. She is also a dancer, and an explorer of body, mind, and spirit.

Esther Perel. Psychotherapist, speaker, and author Esther Perel is recognised as one of the most insightful and provocative voices on personal and professional relationships. Fluent in nine languages, the Belgian native brings a rich multicultural perspective to her clinical practice and workshops. In addition to Esther's thirty-year therapy practice in New York City, she also serves on the faculty of The Family Studies Unit, Department of Psychiatry, New York University Medical Center, and The International Trauma Studies Program at Columbia University. She is also the best-selling author of *Mating in Captivity: Unlocking Erotic Intelligence*, translated into twenty-five languages, and is currently at work on her new book, *The State of Affairs: Cheating in the Age of Transparency*. Her first TED Talk, *The Secret to Desire in Long Term Relationships*, has over 6.5 million views, and her most recent TED, *Rethinking Infidelity*, has been viewed nearly 3 million times since its release in May 2015.

Shinar Pinkas, PhD(C), is principle and senior trainer at Psychosoma, the Post-Graduate Relational Body Psychotherapy School at the Israeli Centre for Body–Mind Medicine. She is a bibliotherapist, body psychotherapist, and supervisor in private practice. Her PhD dissertation (at Bar-Ilan University) explores the absence of the living body in psychoanalysis. Shinar lives in Israel with her partner and two lovely daughters.

Esther Rapoport, PsyD, is a clinical psychologist who maintains a private practice in Tel Aviv. She lectures and writes on gender, sexuality, culture, and psychoanalytic theory. Esther is an incoming Board Member of the Israeli branch of The International Association for Relational Psychoanalysis and Psychotherapy (IARPP), and an active member of Psychoactive—Mental Health Professionals for Human Rights and other activist groups. She is frequently invited by Israeli LGBT organisations to lecture on sensitive care for bisexual and transgender patients. Esther is currently working on a book on bisexuality in psychoanalytic theory and practice, that has been commissioned by a leading academic publisher.

Asaf Rolef Ben-Shahar, PhD, is an Israeli psychotherapist, teacher, and writer. He founded two relational body psychotherapy programmes, in Israel (Psychosoma) and the UK, and is regularly teaching worldwide. Asaf authored two books (*A Therapeutic Anatomy*, Pardes, 2013; *Touching the Relational Edge*, Karnac, 2014) and co-edited with Rachel Shalit *When Hurt Remains—Relational Perspectives on Therapeutic Failure* (Karnac, 2016). He is the editor-in-chief of the International Body Psychotherapy Journal. Asaf is a father to two girls, a novice DJ, bird watcher, and loves dancing and hiking.

John Scofield's guitar work has influenced jazz since the late 1970s and is going strong today. Scofield is a masterful jazz improviser whose music generally falls somewhere between post-bop, funk edged jazz, and R & B. Born in Ohio and raised in suburban Connecticut, Scofield took up the guitar at age eleven, and later attended Berklee College of Music in Boston. After a debut recording with Gerry Mulligan and Chet Baker, he recorded with Charles Mingus, and joined the Gary Burton quartet. He began his international career as a bandleader and recording artist in 1978. Scofield toured and recorded with Miles Davis. Since that time he has prominently led his own groups in the international Jazz scene, recorded over thirty albums as a leader, collaborating and playing with many jazz legends. Touring the world approximately 200 days per year with his own groups, he is an adjunct professor of music at New York University, a husband, and father of two. John won the 2016 Grammy Award for the best jazz instrumental album.

Eyal Shani is an acclaimed Israeli chef, who is a prominent shaper of the culinary scene in Israel. Owner of a few restaurants, as well as providing culinary consultancy, and starring in cooking television shows, Eyal considers food as a substitute for air: he views the world through it, breathes food, and attempts to facilitate happiness in others through food making. He is famous for his passionate and sensual attitude and poetic language to cooking, feeding, and training new chefs.

Trinny Woodall and Susannah Bertelsen are two British fashion advisors, presenters, and authors. They aim to teach women to learn to love themselves from the outside in, to look better, and to feel empowered. In their background they have created their own TV shows—What Not to Wear, on BBC; Undress, The Great British Body, and Trinny & Susannah Meet Their Match, on ITV. Today their TV show Trinny and Susannah – The Makeover Mission, is filmed and aired in twelve countries around the world. Trinny and Susannah also wrote eleven style self-help books that have been published in fifteen countries around the world, and they went on to create their very own clothing and underwear ranges. Although influenced by fashion, they never compromise a woman's individuality by being slaves to fashion, and their purpose is for each woman to discover a newfound feeling of confidence and self-worth.

Silke Ziehl, MSc, is the founder and director of the Entelia Institute for Creative Bodywork. She is an experienced bodyworker and body psychotherapist, an acupuncturist, Hawaiian Huna bodyworker, and a trainer and supervisor in Postural Integration, Energetic Integration, and Pulsing. She has been running bodywork groups and professional training in England, Germany, and Greece for over twenty years. She brings a light touch to deep work, assisting primary processes through attention and non-interference. She has been a member of the Open Centre in London since 1982, is a member of EABP (European Association of Body Psychotherapy), and is current vice president of the International Council of Postural Integration Trainers.

To Tom

Susie Orbach

Speech; the ways we say it, the pauses, the rhythms, the crescendos, the shouts, the sudden silences, the ellipses, whether in sounds or sign language, in gross or subtle physical movements, are the expressions of an embodied self. We are embodied. There is no such thing as a dis-embodied self: that is a tautology.

It is *how* we are embodied that interests the authors of this fine collection. And, as Winnicott would have said it, how our ways of in-dwelling impact on each other and create the loop of engagement that keeps, as John Scofield and Steven Knoblauch eloquently discuss, improvising.

For bodies, like psyches, are made, and they are made in relation-ship. Bodies become vivified by their connection to other bodies. We have known this since Spitz's work in the war wards of infants who died from lack of being psycho-physically related to. Perfunctory care does not a human being make. Failure to thrive, the oft quoted psychological diagnosis of the infant who dies prematurely is often thought of in terms of the mother's (or the nurse's or father's or other's) inability to hold the infant in mind. But this begs the question: how does the infant get held in mind? How does the infant know that he is held in mind? He knows it through his sense of touch, of being held, of being fed, of being changed, of his gaze being received, of the voice he is offered being at a pitch which is responsive and soothing. Psyche for the infant is entwined with body. No infant researcher can talk of mind in anything other than physical turns, and yet the prejudice continues, mind has supremacy.

Accustomed as we are to focusing on minds, and to seeing bodies as a precipitate of mind rather than the outcome of developmental processes that occur between bodies, we neglect to parse bodies in a way we routinely do with psyche. We talk of borderline, dissociated, disorganised, or paranoid–schizoid psyches, with scarcely a thought about bodies except symptomatically. But as these pieces ably show, bodies as bodies are as much the stuff of us as minds, and need understanding no less and no less well than our theories and clinical observations on mind. We can talk of borderline bodies, dissociated bodies, disorganised bodies, paranoid–schizoid bodies. Choose your theory and try rethinking the person you are working with through the lens of the corporeal. Are the psyche and the soma equivalent? Do they diverge? If so why?

What sense can we make developmentally of the history, the bodiography of the individual (The BODI Group Members, 2015)? What do we learn of the bodies that have impacted on and shaped the person's body? What aspects of the maternal/sibling/paternal/cultural body have been physically incorporated in the making of her or his body?

In this impressive and interesting collection there is something for every kind of practitioner. I was moved, as I am sure the reader will be, by many of the pieces, and delighted at the range from the birthing body to the erotic body to the search for a body that can be more than absence and more than pain.

The unique dialogue between the authors offers an exquisite counterpoint. The search to find the right space between, to make offerings from inside of one's own understandings be it spiritual or culinary, serves a delectable repast worth ingesting more than once. The smell, the taste, the feel, the breath, the pain, and the redemptive possibilities of many of these contributions, will surely lead to a collection well-read and talked about. Maybe, even, we shall see the body not as second fiddle but as playing a tune we need to hear.

Introduction

Mustapha Mond and the blue fairy

Throughout his earlier life, Pinocchio's fantasy was to become real; to assume a human form, to have a body. Why bother? Why give up eternity to have a body? Why suffer illness and death, be dependent on our decaying organic matter? Why did Pinocchio make such an effort to become a real live boy?

We are born into bodies; our being is incarnated in the flesh. Our arrival into the world is a highly bodily experience, as is our departure, when our bodily organism ceases to function in a spirited way. And in between, every encounter, every meeting, every relationship, is saturated with us-as-bodies, with sensations, movements, gestures, and perceptions that stem from the body and move through the body. It is part of our developmental task to consciously claim ourselves as bodies.

We are born into bodies but also have to earn our bodyness. Many years after Pinocchio's inevitable death, a conversation took place between one Mr Savage and the world controller Mustapha Mond (in Aldous Huxley's *Brave New World*, 1932). Mr Savage challenged the convenient life held in their world:

"But I don't want comfort. I want God, I want poetry, I want real danger, I want freedom, I want goodness. I want sin".

"In fact," said Mustapha Mond, "you're claiming the right to be unhappy."

"All right then," said the Savage defiantly, "I'm claiming the right to be unhappy".

Taken aback, Mustapha Mond continues to question Savage's desire:

"Not to mention the right to grow old and ugly and impotent; the right to have syphilis and cancer; the right to have too little to eat; the right to be lousy; the right to live in constant apprehension of what may happen to-morrow; the right to catch typhoid; the right to be tortured by unspeakable pains of every kind."

There was a long silence.

"I claim them all," said the Savage at last. (Huxley, 1932, p. 219)

Huxley's Savage strongly claimed his vitality, his spirited freedom, his emancipation. He did that defiantly, but not naively, mindful of the grave price he paid for wanting this freedom, for wanting this body. Pinocchio's quest was similar. Perhaps, to have an idea of what both were so adamantly fighting for, we can turn to phenomenologist Maurice Merleau-Ponty (1962), who argued that the body was our medium for having a world.

Pinocchio wanted to have a world. It was the blue fairy who, by granting him a body, gave him a world. Mr Savage too wanted to have a world; and he needed a body for that. "We become embodied, it seems," wrote body psychotherapist Nick Totton (2005), "in order to temper our being, as a sword is tempered by plunging it red-hot into water. The plunge into matter defines us" (p. 170). These two aspects of our embodiment, the given body and the acquired body, accompany us throughout our lives, and will accompany us throughout this book.

The psychotherapeutic and psychoanalytic encounter engenders deep and meaningful dialogues, fosters growth and curiosity, bringing about change and healing. The three of us, Noa, Liron, and Asaf, have initiated this project out of our shared passion and excitement about bodies and relationships, within therapy and outside of it. Our passion enticed a curiosity: can we bring the body closer to therapy and therapy closer to the body? We sought to bring together the rigour and healing of psychotherapy alongside the creativity and boundlessness of other fields that involve and relate to body. In essence, we wanted to facilitate dialogues about some exciting facets of being-us-as-bodies. We aspired to provide a platform for a meeting of worlds, for cross fertilisation that resulted in an aesthetic, generative, and healing relationship. This book is unique, since it is the fruit of meetings and interactions of people who all share a deep passion and commitment to their embodied being, and invested in supporting others in their journey to become bodies-in-relations. This book is, therefore, a tribute to the blue fairy: it celebrates, mourns, blesses, and sponsors our embodied being and our embodied relating.

To be (a body) or not to be (a body)

That the body is a crucial tenet of the psychotherapeutic process is well accepted today. Yet there is still a gap between contemporary psychoanalytic conceptualisations of the body and their translation into clinical intervention. This too has been changing in the last years (Chodorow, 2012; Cornell, 2008; Knoblauch, 2012; Yarom, 2013 and more).

Psychoanalysis and psychotherapy share the ambiguous and often paradoxical desire to have-a-body and to not-have-a-body, to be-a-body and to not-be-a-body. Much of this paradoxical position is existential, but some of it results from an almost exclusive focus on the body of pathology (or an exclusive focus on the given body and not the acquired body). Freud's drive theory viewed the body (and id) as something to contend with, to tame, to shape, and control. The body as a source of vitality, the body as a portal into connection, the body of bliss—Pinocchio's real body and Mr Savage's—these are strangely missing in most therapeutic doctrines.

In writing this book we wanted to facilitate vital and engaged dialogues about bodies between therapists and non-therapists. Our contributors cordially invite you into some of the deepest, most affective and exciting avenues of psychotherapy and everyday life, at the point where words often lose their meaning and bodies begin to converse.

We divided the book into seven parts, each touching on a different theme of embodiment. We have chosen a few topics that touch on the juxtaposition of body and therapy, but there are many more subjects awaiting exploration. Each theme has a different taste, a different tapestry. Each includes pieces by both contributors (therapist and non-therapist) and a dialogue between them—that is the centrepiece of our book, a place of meeting-of-bodyminds, a place for agreements and arguments, sameness and differentness, and a birthplace of thirdness.

Vignettes from leading figures in psychoanalysis and body psychotherapy explore bodily aspects of sensuality, vitality, beauty, divinity, pain, rhythm, and the therapist's body. Alongside each therapist we can find experts in their respective fields relating to those subjects from their own unique perspective. Thus, each of the seven parts brings the gift of the blue fairy, providing multifaceted attention from various perspectives—philosophical, cultural, aesthetic, and artistic, exploring similar avenues outside therapy. Following the individual pieces, we have hosted a dialogue between the "theme-partners" to weave their views together into a relationship.

In making this book we aspired to create a living project, an embodied enterprise; we sought to create meetings that were both relational and of the body; encounters that celebrate the creation of novelty and are the fruits of dialogue and interaction.

While the individual pieces are the appetisers of each part, the dialogues offer the main courses, offering opportunities for immersing yourself in interdisciplinary voyages into bodies and relationships. These themed discussions awaken and enliven the body in psychotherapy and everyday life.

There is no such thing as a body

Paraphrasing Winnicott (there is no such thing as a body), psychoanalyst Susie Orbach (2003) argued that: "There is also, I suggest, no such thing as a body, there is only a body in relationship with another body" (p. 10). We are introducing you to bodies in relationships with other bodies.

This project was a dialogic journey. We met with many of our contributors, spoke with all; they also spoke among themselves. Some bodies only met via telephone or Skype, others could touch one another. And during the meetings, and the dialogues, we found a quality of aliveness and excitement that was not there before. We found newness, novelty, we found a third. Perhaps, to become real, we all need an other; perhaps we need relationships in order to embody, and bodies in order to relate. Perhaps we are all Pinocchio seeking the blue fairy's blessings, and at the same time we are the blue fairy, blessing others and making them real with our blessing.

We hope that you find this project inspiring and vitalising, and we welcome comments, feedback, and further dialogue and correspondence:

Asaf Rolef Ben-Shahar: asaf@imt.co.il
Liron Lipkies: lironfanti@hotmail.com
Noa Oster: noa_oster@yahoo.com

PART I

THE RHYTHMIC BODY

Introduction to Part I

L iron Lipkies (2012) suggested that "There are moments where words do not serve us well, and the language of the body is the most appropriate one to use" (p. 53). This is true, of course, not just for psychotherapy, since somatic communication constitutes a significant agent in any relationship. However, what do we attend to as psychotherapists in those moments? Sensations and tonality, musculature and breathing, gestures and positioning, have been central to body psychotherapy theory and practice, and also explored in psychoanalysis.

As soon as we attend to bodily functions we encounter rhythms and pulsation. Human interaction requires constant improvisation, attunement to self and other, and misattunement, oscillating between togetherness and separateness in the attempt to create something meaningful, aesthetic, valuable; very much like jazz.

We have therefore invited two jazz players to talk about rhythm. Relational psychoanalyst Steven Knoblauch has substantially written about rhythm, jazz, and psychoanalysis (e.g., 1997, 1999, 2000, 2005, 2012), and he wrote a piece that explores the unfolding relational rhythms in analysis through a fascinating case study. John Scofield, one of the most renowned guitarists alive today and a prolific creator, artist, and jazz musician, has joined Steven in a dialogue, speaking of improvisation, analysis, rhythm, and failure.

To maintain the jazz quality of the dialogue, John has not written an individual piece but has directly joined in a dialogue with Steven, his friend of over forty years. We have intentionally preserved the improvisational and rhythmic quality of their dialogue to present to you a jam session, bouncing ideas off one another, and demonstrating the value of rhythm in analytic thinking and practice, and certainty—in any human communication.

CHAPTER ONE

Polyrhythmic weave of micro-moment interaction

Steven H. Knoblauch

E yes squint, cheeks puff just slightly, chin sharpens, forehead tightens, lips moving slowly, then shifting as tones become more pronounced . . . quiet facial rhythms out of tempo, striving for synchrony . . . all collapse into flared nostrils. "Sheeee . . . keeeeps . . . texxxxxxting meeeee . . . it's driiiiiiiving me craaaaaaazyy . . . I'm in the middle of work . . . I can't take this!!!" A rolling out of words in legato, but with increasing crescendo settling into seven then four crisp accents. With Tony's face and words, a tap dance of tentative testing for some secure ground on which to feel safe, a place of protection from the avalanche of emotion his girlfriend is unleashing in the middle of a work day, a staccato chatter of text messages bombarding Tony's mobile phone. It is hard to tell if Tony is more scared than angry, but clearly some of both in this facial eruption here/now. As he speaks feelings (his and his girlfriend's), clouds of an emotional storm between and within Tony and me begin to shape the space and horizons of our encounter.

Chest muscles tightening, legs and back shift me slightly to the edge of my chair. My breathing seems to speed up, but as I train my focus, this rhythm slows to accompany the visual effort I am intending with Tony. I do not feel angry with him, or scared for, or of, him at this point, but rather suspended in a pause . . . a place of uncertainty . . .

of not really knowing what is going on emotionally . . . for Tony . . . between Tony and me. My visual effort to vigilantly track the (e)motion in the room is cross modally entrained to the kind of buildup of feeling Tony seems to be experiencing. Out on the edge of awareness, I somehow sense my own effort to meet him in the gathering of this storm. But, I am also aware of how stuck we seem to be at a certain point of this not-so-unfamiliar-arrangement, this scene of frustration. Here Tony seems to reach out to me for some kind of strength and clarity, a magic bullet for navigating the unpredictable, vexing . . . no more than that . . . infuriating . . . narcissistic demands of his girlfriend whom he has described, at other points, as an intimate partner deeply attuned and responsive to his needs.

Multiple streams of entry begin to fill and flood my reverie as we sit in a dark cloud of silence . . . a powerful pause. I am remembering descriptions of Tony's father's passivity, his seeming inability to recognise the emotional states and needs of his wife or son. I am remembering descriptions of Tony's mother's meddlesome intrusiveness, suffocating possibilities for the recognition of, or expression of, her child's wishes, fears, hopes, and dreams.

Tony often seems unable to experience wishes, fears, hopes, and dreams with me or otherwise. His pursuit of extreme sports seems, at times, to constitute a search for the thresholds of where fear might be discovered, as if those internal fears with which he is constantly haunted, demanded such effort. These states are often difficult, if not impossible to recognise for Tony. When we talk about his work, he is preoccupied with protecting it as a place of retreat and our focus concerns how to avoid being labelled a failure and/or scapegoat. This pattern occurs repeatedly, early in the treatment. He fears moving out of one dysfunctional family into another, taking the same role in a repeating dramatic scene. And yet, as treatment progresses, Tony begins to find ways to establish his competence at work, to take leadership and to transfer into a new work group (family) where he is no longer being made a scapegoat. He even begins to allow himself to hope and dream of more responsibility, better income, and a sense of direction to his personal and professional life trajectory, a sustained lively rhythm of anticipation different than the tempos of our conversations early in treatment.

But here, in this moment of encounter . . . after several attempts to find safety and relatedness with Gail, from whom he often recoils as if hitting a wall of emotional anesthesia . . . again . . . Tony is wrestling with the angels of intimacy . . . of having his own needs and feelings recognised and responded to . . . of learning to recognise and respond to those of another whom he would cherish. Over and over again he has described many scenes of pleasure, playfulness, and a growing sense of intimate companionship with Gail. But here is the other Gail, desperate "nagging", triggering, or in response to, Tony's unpredictable retreats into emotional anesthesia that he is now bringing to me. What does Tony want . . . confirmation of his feelings . . . help in managing the difficult tensions of intimacy . . . an exit strategy to once again avoid being smothered and controlled by a monster mother? Confusion and breakdown are now threatening us. Will we meet and survive Tony's anger? This is the kind of anger from his father that scared him away . . . the kind of anger that triggers in Tony a fear that he will destroy or be destroyed emotionally . . . a helpless prisoner . . . never to see the light of freedom to pursue his own unique dreams and wishes. But could this also be a kind of storm that may help liberate him from his emotional anesthesia?

Will I be destroyed by Tony's anger? Suspended in my reflective pause, I am opening up an unexpected syncopation to the rhythms of our exchange. How will Tony experience this unexpected shift in tempo? How will my inability to find words of comfort or safety, at least in this moment, affect how Tony will feel? Does he experience my pause as confusion . . . as retreat . . . as defeat? Or might this break in the building crescendo of feelings in the air open a wide chasm . . . but as a space for something new to emerge?

All of the sudden, Tony's mobile phone rings. He hesitates. He shifts his gaze from phone to my face back to phone. The brief meeting of our gazes is staggered and chaotic . . . I experience confusion and desperation. My sense is that Tony is mightily drawn to answer that call and deeply fears being seduced into a masochistic moment of defeat to an all devouring, monstrous Other who cannot recognise and respect a space for his need to work, his unique needs for play, his own need to be in a safe therapeutic space with me. I am both wanting to act to help, and feeling confident that I should remain still and not speak, lest I become a manifestation of non-recognition and disrespect (my not trusting Tony's capacity to manage his emotions here could contribute to his inability to trust his own emotional response and how he might communicate it). So I hold open space for

Tony's experience to coalesce into something he can recognise . . . something he can feel recognised.

Tony's face tightens again, muscles gathering steam, building a fiery red anger. He speaks. "IT'S HERRRRRRRRRR." The words explode as bass accents heralding doom. Internally, I hear the first four notes of Beethoven's Fifth Symphony, but then the emphatic call, no, cry, for attention to a cross-generationally transmitted suffering from generations of cruelty and oppression, the opening phrases of Rahsaan Roland Kirk's *Inflated Tear*. I am still in internal reverie, a fleeting second overflowing acoustic imagery, carrying so much meaning. Now comes thought, at least brief reflections. I wonder about the suffering of Tony's parents, of his parents' parents, of the cruelty and oppression, collective, familial, cross-generational patterns transmitting expectations for trauma. I wonder about the feelings of psychic annihilation that could be visiting Tony. Will he explode in anger or anesthetise, contracting into dissociation? Can he find in Gail . . . in me . . . in anyone . . . some recognition and responsiveness to his emotional states that can help these states to exist for Tony to recognise and use, and not dissolve into dissociation?

My confusion . . . my pause . . . my disruption of our rhythm could be so disorganising . . . so creating a sense of non-responsiveness, of non-recognition from me . . . in Tony. But, my pause also seems to open up a syncopation for emotional resonance with Tony. It is as if his baritone saxophone is initiating a wave of energy, a vibration of air, rhythm, tone, and accent crossing the room. As in a tsunami, my cello is swept up resonantly in this rushing energy, becoming engulfed with a similar expectation/fear for experiences of anger, confusion, and self-doubt hesitation. But, this wave moving at light speed between, also precipitates a shift of recognition in my subjectivity, particularly in my face. I am touched, no, shaken, but at the same time awakened. This burst of activation paradoxically shakes me into a state, calm and receptive. Though still with uncertainty, I am not frightened away. I do not panic with some kind of action that might feel like usurpation or attack in a moment when Tony needs to find his own agency. I have known Tony for years. I have a deep compassion for him and his suffering and I have seen him grow slowly through such crises. My forehead seems less creased than his, my cheeks less inflated, my mouth slightly open, nostrils and breath in a repeating, slowing rhythm (Knoblauch, 2011, 2012). I look directly into Tony's face and wait.

Tony too is quiet. He looks down at the buzzing mobile phone. He does not answer. He looks up at me. There is a moment of inquiry with less confusion in his gaze. His quickly shifting rhythm is not in any recognisable cadence, almost as if he is feeling his way through different states of emotion, testing and sensing his own various capacities for retreat, attack, or something else. I cannot say for sure what that something else might be. Our words do not represent our experiences. Speaking is an inadequate metaphor for abstraction and containment. Rather as this pause stretches out, the colour in Tony's face reduces in intensity. The previous glare in his eyes softens and settles into a downward gaze. (Sometimes the floor or wall or somewhere "out there" can provide an effective mirror for internal reflection.) Tony is self-soothing, calming. He will not destroy or be destroyed by Gail or me. The space created by our shifting and syncopating our rhythms from accelerating staccato accents of percussive strength into a long pause creates a moment of recognition and agency for Tony.

What had just happened?

My own sense of this, clearly shaped by a particular style of attention and relating in analytic encounters, is that critical emotional navigation was occurring both within and between Tony and me on dimensions of embodied rhythmic patterning (see Knoblauch, 2011 for examples). Sensing acceleration, deceleration, of pause, accent, and syncopation became the critical registration and communication both for and between each of us. This is not, in any way, to devalue the words and meanings we were also using to communicate. Here I want to emphasise that words can serve a representational or symbolic function, communicating various meanings that mark and distinguish experience for shared understanding. But words are also embodied with tone and accent, non-representational dimensions carrying deeply emotional meaning and interpersonal influence (Bucci, 1997, p. 194). Here, the enacted dimensions of a clinical encounter are not to be understood in some kind of bifurcated conceptualisation as one pole of which understanding is the other. Rather, enactments can be experienced as a continuation of the co-creation of emotionally significant meaning both preceding, as the medium for, and in response to, other symbolic forms of communication and influence as with words. Thus, the rhythms of speaking emerge from within an array of embodied tempos registered as breathing, movement of limbs and torso, and especially formations of gaze and facial display, and including the impact of internal processes such as blood pressure and other embodied changes that impact skin colour, sound, taste, touch, sight sensations, and so on. From this perspective, enactment in a clinical encounter is constituted by two rhythmic bodies weaving complex, polyrhythmic patterning often occurring on micro-dimensions of the exchange, and always carrying and carried by significant emotional navigation.

The above observations are important because patients come to us with a repertoire of rhythmic patterning scaffolding their emotional relationships. This is patterning having its origins in varying activities and varying periods of any individual's life as it unfolds, as well as the present moment of interaction. This polyrhythmic patterning is simultaneously emerging and learned, entrained, as Trevarthen (1998), Stern (1985, 2004, 2010), and others have suggested, from as early as intrauterine experience. And so it is on this level of interaction that cross generationally transmitted trauma, but also pragmatic learning, connects our histories, presence, and anticipated futures through polyrhythmic patterning that can be significant to our personal lives, and in particular, for the purpose of emphasis here, how we experience and relate in our clinical encounters with patients.

CHAPTER TWO

Dialogue: the song that's in our head

Steven H. Knoblauch, John Scofield,
Asaf Rolef Ben-Shahar, Liron Lipkies, and Noa Oster

E ditors: Will you speak about the connection between music and therapy?

Steven Knoblauch: I came to music as a little boy listening to the radio. I used to kind of dance around in my mom's kitchen listening to Elvis Presley and all the tunes that were on the local radio station. I think the linkage between music and therapy is the motion, (e)motion is a funny word because if you take away the e you have motion, and what is so beautiful about music is that it galvanises emotions, expresses emotions that you already have, giving them greater clarity and expression. And it always comes with breath, in and out, and in movement, and it has different speeds and different waves in which it breaks up like rhythm. So, as I walk down the street or as I interact with people in my office, I am always aware that there is an emotion being created, a wave of feeling, even if we sit silently there is a wave of feelings. Sometimes that wave can be a quiet one and at other times very loud.

John Scofield: I really like in Steven's writing the way he talks about music, especially musical disciplines where we use improvisation, and perhaps the key element is improvisation, something that we use all the time in life, that's how we get through life. When I'm trying to teach jazz I always say that it's exactly what we do when we are thinking and talking. You come up with ideas spontaneously, and a lot of those ideas are things that you thought about and used before . . . like language, we repeat ourselves all the time and the human condition involves change and things happening before . . . and we are always responding in the moment . . . a lot of people don't understand how you can improvise music when they think about how hard it is to play an instrument, yet it's the same thing we do in life every day, just using our mind as our instrument.

Eds: Can you say something about the place of improvisation in communication, perhaps also in music and psychotherapy?

JS: Steven, do you want to handle that one?

SK: Yeah . . . I am not so sure that it is so easy to sort out, because I like the way John describes improvisation as something that is innate to being. We learn language through being with others who speak that language and it just becomes part of our mind and our body, so we don't reflect on it and say "I'm improvising", we simply respond. For example, we are improvising right now, I didn't get a script, I don't know what I'm going to say next, John doesn't know what he is going to say in response to your questions; we are improvising and feeling maybe a little anxious at times, a little confirmed at times, a little elated at other times, so we're going through those emotional waves . . . I think maybe the difference between therapy and what we are doing now is that in treatment we try to focus on areas of pain. A patient comes to us and we are ready to receive an experience of moving to an area that is painful, that involves the history of suffering. Suffering has its own kind of rhythms. It's more difficult to do. That's why it's different than common language, but improvisation runs across all modes of interaction . . . let me stop there.

JS: That's great Steven, and I think that in improvisation of all types, we are using material that we have rehearsed and thought of for a long time, so it's not like you are always coming up with stuff that's new . . . Occasionally you will come up with putting things together in a way that you haven't done before, I guess nothing is new . . . in personal relationships or in music . . . so we are using our whole essence when we improvise, our whole musical essence, just as I'm talking to you right now and improvising. And sometimes you have a script, the great thing about jazz is we are able to get away from the script in that kind of music more than in other kinds of music, and it's just a little closer to real life[1] . . . maybe that's why jazz has been successful and spread far and wide.

SK: I would like to pick up on couple of things . . . a really important point John makes is how difficult it is, even though we are improvising, to come up with something new . . . as we are improvising here, we are using words that we used many times before, and at some point we had to learn how to formulate and how to string words and sentences together. Musical language is similar. But as he also points out, when you're improvising, you're in a place where you put words and phrases together maybe in a new kind of way every once in a while, a radically new kind of way. And so the significance of improvisation for therapeutic work is in our striving for breakthroughs, we are striving for new formulations for ourselves and for our patients, and that's the work of therapeutic growth. The other thing I wanted to pick up on is the healing of improvisation, both in music and in psychoanalysis. There is something incredibly healing both for the player and for the audience, which is why I think people are so drawn to music and it is such a central part of life, and how and why it's such an important dimension of therapeutic work, paying attention to rhythms; paying attention to tone, to the emotional surges, to the crescendos and decrescendos that structure any interaction, any analytic engagement.

JS: I think it's awesome . . . makes me wonder about how as therapists you deal with everybody's on the split-second emotional wave, when you are working with someone. Because you must be aware that there is all this unseen stuff that happens to the therapist and the patient, just like the different musicians in a band when we're trying to get it together and with the audience, so there are all these connections . . . maybe I'm wrong but they seem too quick and too special for me to even understand . . . That we are just communicating with each other, on such a quick intuitive level, where our whole being is picking up of each other and ourselves . . . And that's really true in playing music with other people, or in playing for an audience—the response you get from other people who are listening to you, where you can tell somehow in a room if you are going over, even without the applause, you can feel it, and what are all these waves of communication between humans? I know Steven thought about this a lot. You all have.

Eds: As you speak we notice the balance between structure and rhythms, flow and form. The two of you take turns in a highly interesting way. One of you finishes and the other picks up the thread; you seem to hand it over to each other. Perhaps it's important to note that you know each other for many years, that you are friends, that you have a relationship.

JS: Steve, I'm just gonna go first for a second . . . When we play music that's really true, we are improvising together, and it is so related to how you feel about the other person . . . If you feel friendly and on the same wavelength, you can play together . . . But sometimes you'll play things that might block what makes you feel comfortable musically, somebody else will play stuff, which seems to get in your way, and that can make it more difficult to work, and at the same time if you play well with somebody and you know you can make music together almost always the interpersonal relationships are easy[2] . . . and this has always surprised me, that when I have a musical bond with somebody, even if I don't know him that well, and then I get to know him from playing together, even when I realise this guy is a really different person than I am, and normally in the real world we wouldn't be friends but the music has brought us together because we can communicate this way . . . go ahead Steven . . . you got it.

Eds: We have a little flash on the screen whenever someone wants to start speaking . . . and you (John) said to Steven: "Go ahead Steven you've got it" just as Steven breathed, before he even began talking . . . How did you know that he wanted to speak?

JS: Well I didn't know he wanted to speak . . . I just ran out of ideas.

SK: Well we're on the same wave . . . We are a good band. You mentioned earlier structure and flow and I think about the pause . . . and a pause has a kind of texture about it, and tension—and this tension is important as it creates an opening . . . and there's a language in rhythm and pauses. I feel like with my pet dog the music connects us so we understand each other, but I don't believe my dog really understands English, I sure don't understand Dogish . . . Similarly, there is a rhythm that we feel with people when we are attracted sexually or otherwise.

They pick up on some kind of rhythm in us. Rhythm is timing. It can create or dissolve structure and flow. Rhythm changes shift into possibilities, slowing down or speeding up, right John?

JS: Yeah. . .

SK: If you would shift into playing slow, others would feel the shift and move into the new rhythm with you.

JS: We are trying to use all the possibilities that we know of . . . trying to learn more possibilities, more shapes that you can apply. Space is a really good thing too . . . really important . . . pausing and letting things change. Everything is just changing all the time, so sometimes if you put a little pause there, everybody's awareness comes up. If you stop speaking or playing for a moment . . . others' thoughts come through and that in turn changes the situation a little bit . . . and good jazz musicians are very aware of this music-space . . . What musicians do when they practise is just play all the time, but when you actually perform you have to breathe . . . and you space that dramatic pause, which we use all the time in life . . . like now . . . and this is what you do when you are working with somebody as therapists . . . [pause] and then sometimes there's too much space, just like here . . . [laughs]

Eds: Looking at your attunement to one another, we were wondering if you can imagine having chosen one another's paths . . . Steven would have become a full time jazz musician and John if you will have taken your skills into therapeutic or analytic work.

JS: Wow . . . I guess that would mean I wouldn't have to go on the road all the time . . . get to stay home more. Life could have gone in a bunch of different ways . . . certainly Steven could have stayed with music and perfected that and be very successful. We use creativity and improvisation in everything, every day of our lives . . . Everybody has to use improvisation, like communicating with other people, so that we are not just alone.

SK: In many ways you can say that the work of any healing, as a therapist or analyst, is to help patients to learn and improvise in their lives, with their children or others, to learn to navigate the tensions between flow and structure.

Eds: That reminds us of Winnicott (1971) saying that if a patient cannot play they need to be taught to play before commencing any other work. Can we shift to speak about bodies? You were talking about breathing, John, can you speak about the body in improvisation?

JS: I think music really is just a reflection of nature . . . and I never thought that until I wondered about what are these notes and these rhythms and these sounds. They seemed to reflect the world we live in. Like nature and the order of things . . . when you look at other creations, trees, and flowers, and plants, when you just open your eyes and look at what's around you and our body is part of that, part of the world . . . and when I'm playing, a lot of the music that comes out of me, or any music, is probably related to the breathing and to the whole living organism, it's coming through me . . . It's a lot like being a singer, what you are trying to do on that instrument is the same that you do when you sing . . . and we realise when we sing that it's just coming from our body, from our organism . . . So I'm connected to my body, my guitar is connected to my body through my hands, you know they always say it's an extension of the body . . . but it really is for all of us . . . Go ahead.

SK: I was thinking about how much learning how to play has to do with being around people, and seeing how they play their instruments . . . somebody was studying the way musicians move and how much it had to do with the expression of their playing. You (John) have a very unique way of moving when you play. Your body moves with the music—it expresses your crescendos, and when you play higher or as you are playing something softer, you can almost see your body accompanying the sound, it's almost like the instrument is an expression of what your body is experiencing and expressing . . . it is you but it's not just you, and almost any great musician if you think: Keith Jarrett playing piano or Chick Corea, there is a way in which they move their body . . . or the way Miles plays trumpet . . . You can see how their movements are so distinctive to the way they express themselves. Even with classical musicians, the body is intrinsically involved in the creation of sound. There is a parallel there, as we speak, as we relate, we know from infant researchers [For example, see Trevarthen, 2009; Trevarthen & Aitken, 2001] that our face, our tone of voice, the way we move our body: leaning forward, using our hands, all of that is part of the ensemble of our emotional experience, not just what the words represent, it's not just the ability to move from a primary process to a secondary process. That to me is a false binary.

Eds: We have watched you play, John, and often it seems that the music begins to play you rather then you playing the music . . . and there is a surrender to something. Both in music and also in deep analytic moments there is surrender to something that's bigger than us, and if we are successful then that very surrender has a real aesthetic and transformative quality.

JS: That's true . . . When you learn how to play jazz and you get better at it . . . Some people say "I feel like I'm not really playing", that something else happened and I surrender . . . what I think it is, is that we all have a song going in our head, we always do, and all you have to do is play that song. And when you get good on your instrument it just comes through, just like words, like I'm speaking right now . . . And you surrender to that flow, and sometimes it is better than what you can think of when you slow it down, the stuff that comes out spontaneously is better than the things you could compose. And I think that you do surrender . . . Your body is like a little puppet because you are just going with the improvisation, going with the music . . . And this is one of the big mysteries, where does this stuff come from.

SK: The idea that our bodies are almost always more than what we usually define ourselves . . . One way of thinking about this is the idea of surrender, but it's only a part of it. It's that song in our head, the way you put it John. It's also like when you and Bill Stewart and Steve Swallow are playing together . . . What you are playing happens because you are playing with Bill and Steve, in part . . . Obviously you have a tune in mind, you start with that, but then what happens depends on these relationships.

JS: Yes, we're responding to what's around us.

SK: So that, who we are—that unfolding song—is constantly us and also surrendering to something greater which starts with the interaction with those around us. Which is, I think, the richness of what we tap into when we surrender in psychoanalysis . . . The more we can surrender, the more in-tune or in flow we are with our patients and with the emotional moments that shape our encounter.

JS: You know, one thing in jazz is that we study music all the time . . . We study improvisation, you study what music is, and you try to internalise the music so you know more, so you have more in you, and then you improvise . . . At the end of the day you take what you know and you let it come out. And it comes out on its own. You can force it, but really the best is when you're just letting it come through you, and that song that's in your head is coming out of your body and you are improvising along with what the others are saying . . . That's what we're doing in our interactions with people all the time.

Eds: So what do we do when it doesn't work?

JS: Abort! What do we do when it doesn't work . . . this is a good question! You know what, it doesn't always work, does it? Sometimes I play with Phil Lesh, the base player from Grateful Dead, and he has a microphone hooked up that only goes through the monitor and it doesn't go to the audience . . . and he tells us what key to go to, and sometimes he'll just completely improvise he'll say "go to B". And sometimes he yells into the microphone "Abort" . . . [laughing], and that's true in improvisation. And you know, you do the best you can. Your mind goes to the next possible phase you can possibly do, and you don't sweat it because it's never perfect. That's one of the great things about jazz is that you have *license to make mistakes* because of course it's improvisation so there has to be times when it doesn't work . . . Some of the greatest jazz performances include mistakes where everybody sort of screws up for a minute, but because you are professional you are pretty good in making it work . . . you don't have to stop . . . you move on the next thing. And the way that you make it less painful is that you realise that you are gonna screw up. Every night I am going to make mistakes. If I listen to my playing, every phrase has mistakes in it and ways that I wish I hadn't played . . . But also every phrase has little interesting things that are not quite staged, and these open up new opportunities . . . And sometimes it's the little mis-notes and subtleties that I didn't even intend to do that make my mind immediately see another way. If I play everything the way I wanted to play it, none of those things would happen . . . So the improviser, just like the human being, uses these little mistakes in order to find a different direction and a new slightly different way, which may be that mistake . . . so we have to be open to that.

SK: John, the statement that you made captures the essence of therapy, it could be a metaphor for good therapy—taking into consideration the vulnerability of the analyst and also the *ways* that we have to take into account that vulnerability—anticipate ruptures and look for ways to repair, which often bring the most creative moments in jazz and in our work . . . I can also tell another story when John was playing in his first recording and he made mistakes there . . . And yet that performance contributed to his getting recognised.

JS: That's true . . . Yeah, in the first record I ever played on I made a big mistake and it's on the record . . . Not that many people noticed as I would have thought . . . But the other good stuff that was happening overshadowed it even though I was not aware of it . . . and I think it must be the same for you as healers—you can't be too self-aware, we have to allow the process to just keep happening, that's when the good stuff is gonna happen.

Eds: Thank you both, you have been so in-tune or so in-flow with one another, and we were thinking how great it would have been if we as therapists were able to adopt some of the humility of jazz improvisation in their inevitable permission to make mistakes.

SK: Yes, John has just captured in many ways the essence of our work. Thank you.

Notes

1. Interesting to note the similarity to relational conceptualisation of analysis as closer to "real relationships" than it was previously held (Aron & Starr, 2013; Mitchell, 2000, 2005).
2. A beautiful way of noting the importance of both attunement and mis-attunement in interaction.

PART II

THE LIVING BODY

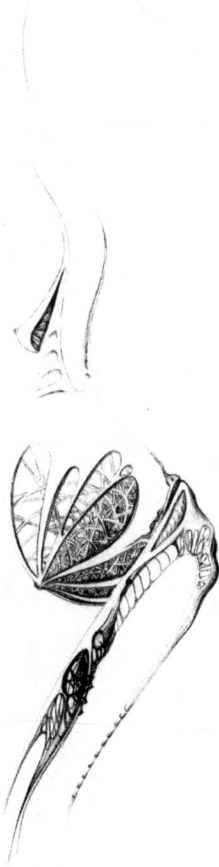

Introduction to Part II

F ounder of bioenergetics, Alexander Lowen (1965), wrote:

> For too long, Western thought has regarded the body as a mechanism,
> an instrument of the will, or a repository of the spirit. Modern medi-
> cine, for all its advances, still holds to this view. We do not take our
> bodies seriously except when something goes wrong. (p. 316)

As we come to discuss the living body, we wish to look at the vitality inherent to us by virtue of being embodied organisms. Our sensing and breathing, our capacity to move, our health and our illness,
are embodied relatedness—all these make for the tapestry of our
aliveness and our being.

We have invited two women to engage with this theme. Body
psychotherapist and bodyworker Silke Ziehl, who has trained many
generations of body psychotherapists in Europe, weaves her personal
and professional perspectives on awareness and aliveness. Janet
Balaskas, who created Active Birth and is one of the foremost activists
for promoting and supporting natural birth in the UK and worldwide,
writes on the birthing body, and discusses the immanent wisdom of

body that manifests through the birthing process. Following their individual pieces, Janet and Silke met with our editorial team. They discuss their papers, vitality, and spirituality. Naturally, these also bring with them the shadow aspects of aliveness, including fear and deadness.

CHAPTER THREE

A body in relationship

Silke Ziehl

What is a living body? Images come up in my mind, memories.

His body was barely breathing. He lay under the lamps, kept warm, kept in a coma, his life in the balance. My little grandson. But I could not feel him, could not make that connection to the life force, the spirit within him.

Another memory. I held him in my arms, close to my body (kangaroo care they call it in Great Ormond Street Hospital). He is looking at me. Intensely. His little head has colourful wires sticking to it all around, measuring his brain activity. But it is his gaze that I am caught by. We look at one another for a very long time, slowly meeting. We are related.

For months, his little body found peace only when tightly held, wrapped, swaddled. Any movement, even his own arm moving, would startle and frighten him. Terror was never far away. Having been that close to death, his body carried terror close to the skin, ready to jump any moment. With time, and calm and loving care, the terror decreased. His body could cope with more, bit by bit—with movements, with surprises, with noises.

The damage to his brain has been harder to change. Large areas of his brain melted in those few hours of high fever shortly after birth. Many upper body reflexes and movements were destroyed, leaving his left arm out of his body-awareness and at first he was unable to move it. His swallowing and digesting reflexes were severely handicapped, his body as a whole quite uncoordinated.

But he was alive, in the deepest sense that I understand it: there was an intense desire to relate, to make contact, to make an impact, to be treated as a person; there was spirit and soul in this body. He could not speak words—but his eyes spoke and his body spoke—and people all around related to him as a person.

Now, six years later, he is using sign language, though he would much rather talk. He has learned to walk and is now aware of and able to move his left arm. He can throw a ball with both hands. He has grown: he is looking over the kitchen worktops at me, his little head bobbing up and down as he walks, following his dad. He is still severely handicapped, and often in pain. Yet he is very much a person, with powerful intentions, likes and dislikes, the ability to learn, and a strong wish to communicate and to relate. And very much alive.

Another memory from another time. Helping at a school fête of my daughter's infant school, I am lifting little kids onto the back of a pony so they can have a ride. I learn a very important lesson that afternoon: there is barely any relationship at all between the measurable size and weight of a child's body and the effort I have to expend to lift that body onto the pony.

Some scrawny little girl was almost impossible for me to lift—she seemed glued and screwed to the ground. Yet a big and heavy looking girl double her size took no effort at all to lift up—in fact she seemed to glide onto the pony under her own steam. Objective weight counted for much less than the child's emotion and desire in determining my effort.

In martial arts, this ability of the alive body to change its own quality, presence, and action potential with changing thoughts and intentions is key. To feel the difference of power and impact of a "normal" arm change into the "unbendable" arm with just a change of thinking and its resultant bodily changes of being is always stunning. When the thinking changes from one of resistance to the other to one of total focus on the goal intended, the physical ability of the arm changes dramatically. It seems like magic to a mind caught up in Cartesian thinking and the separation of body and mind.

As a bodyworker and body-psychotherapist, I see my role mainly as helping clients to befriend their bodies. That is, to reconnect to those previously excluded and forgotten aspects of their aliveness with curiosity and interest, with kindness. And to include whatever is found into the rich and complex fabric of their self-awareness and self-acceptance.

> Tamara had joined a longer training. I had worked with her before, valued her rich experience. On the first day of the training, she suddenly jumped up, gathered her shoes, and ran for the door. I do not normally stop people from leaving, but something in her manner made me jump up and stand in front of the door, refusing to let her run out of the room. It took a while.
>
> I spoke to the part that was running away, and I also spoke to the adult woman. It became clear that a very young part had got very frightened and hijacked the body to run away from danger. Talking with the adult woman helped her to come back into the body. Together, we could calm the young part. Tamara stayed the whole course and was glad I had not let that young part of her rush out without checking with her mature adult part first.

Sometimes life experiences bring the bodymind into a state where death seems close. As it was with my grandson. As it was with Tamara. Such experiences leave their trace in the body. Under stress, the old fear patterns of fight, or flight, or freeze may suddenly erupt, usurping the body.

It is important at such times to bring the body back from the hyper-reactivity that engulfs it and leaves the brain less able to function with its full capacity.

> Pam stood very still. Standing beside her, I felt unsure, felt in the wrong place, and I could not breathe properly. "Where would you like me to stand?" I asked. She could not say. So I waited. "Here," she said, pointing to her left side. I moved there—but still, I could not feel at rest. "Is that the right distance? Or shall I move a bit further away?" "Yes, a bit further away," she said, hesitantly . . ..
>
> By the time we had found the place for me where she could relax and feel safe, I was standing at the farthest away point in the room, looking away from her. Then, finally, it felt safe enough for her to be with me and be with herself, at peace. Standing there, finally, I could breathe

easily. And Pam could start paying attention to herself, and to talk to me about what she found in her body, what she wanted me to know.

Over the years I have learned to honour the body's knowing and the body's talking, both the client's body and my own body. I have learned to trust that a client will be able to find what will help him or her to become more aware—aware of what he or she needs and wants and does not want. If given time and permission, and sometimes encouragement, paying attention to their body's talking they will find the next step, the next clue, on their journey of discovery.

I see my role as therapist as a role of holding the space and giving time. And bringing my conscious awareness and my somatic awareness, listening to my body, being willing to resonate with the client's aliveness and the client's bodymind—and to share that awareness with the client.

When a person can feel safe enough with and welcomed enough by another human being, they can pay attention to aspects of their lives, their body, which had been frozen, forgotten or excluded from awareness. Those aspects can then be brought back from oblivion, can be acknowledged and integrated into the web of their life-experiences. They can be woven back into the fabric of the story of their life, no longer condemned to be undigested and unintegrated residues floating barely connected in psychic space.

The role of the therapist as witness to what the client is exploring is very important. The therapist's attention and witnessing allows the client to look anew, with fresh eyes so to say, to listen with attentive and kind ears, to their own unfolding story—and not to get caught up in old critical patterns or self-attacking habits. The kind and witnessing attention allows aliveness back in the tissues, allows the flames of life to grow stronger. Criticism and attack weaken the flame of life, threaten new sparks, deaden the soul.

I use my own body as a resonance chamber. I allow myself to "open the doors" and let the client's energies flow into and through me. In so doing, I also allow the client to "check me out"—to get an idea of who I am and whether I am safe to be with. In fact, when working with touch and contact, the very first action I do is to just wait, doors open, and invite the client to check me out. Only then will I ask permission to start sinking a bit deeper into their energetic space, allowing myself to "get a bodily felt sense of their reality".

By paying attention to my own body, its signals and messages, I can often learn something about the client's body and reality. If I cannot breathe easily, it is likely that the client is in a similar state. If I cannot relax, often the client is unable to do so, too. For when we are together in the therapeutic space, we share that space and the energies within it. Like currents of air, we mingle. Intersubjectivity is first and foremost a bodily experience. At any moment however, either one or both of us can pull back, unmingle, close the door.

Paradoxically, in order to connect deeply, we need to have good and clear boundaries that allow us to know our own power and agency. Unless I can say No and Yes, I cannot connect to another. Unless I grant myself my own power of agency, I am not able to enjoy another's being and otherness.

> The first time I saw Joey, I was struck by the way he held his head: always with his neck slightly bent forward, eyes never looking directly at me. His voice was soft, his whole demeanour was soft and sweet. I had a fantasy image of a very young boy who was very much in love with his mummy.

> Joey and I had a lovely journey of "playing with anger"—for real anger was just so far away in his inner world that the only way was playing with it. At first we made stories around furry animals and play fights between them. Later we had play fights with cushions. And stories of real people and real concerns, with conflicting goals. Over time, Joey started looking me in the eye. He stood taller. His voice changed and became fuller. His shoulders seemed squarer. He was able and willing to have a different opinion, to accept conflict, and look for a resolution without giving in. I became aware that I felt that I was in the presence of a very lovely man, who was able and willing to stand his ground and had a sense of his own male power. And who was very much alive in his body.

A living body is a body constantly in movement, however small. And it is a body that is constantly sending out tendrils of awareness, messages of communication, to those around. Like cells, we need others to stay aware and alive. We need others to confirm our humanity, our view of reality, our sense of ourselves, and our sense of the world around us. We need others in order to become more of ourselves. And the deeper we allow ourselves to connect, to ourselves, and to others, the more alive we are.

CHAPTER FOUR

A birthing body

Janet Balaskas

W e are bodies.

Over the years I have come to perceive myself as an organism, a magnificent organism as we all are, which includes myriads of systems—the internal systems for living, breathing, digesting, moving, the amazing things we can do with our bodies, and an incredible mind that informs our body. I see us as very interesting vital bio-organisms. We are strongly connected to gravity; we may think of the difference between us and a tree as our ability to move our roots, change our position and move as a way of expressing ourselves—through our body. Our physiology is designed for movement.

I did not always feel like this. When I was much younger I was afraid of my feelings, I was afraid of just everything, I did not have the sense of connection I currently have with my body. Now, as I am approaching my seventies, as a human being I feel more vibrant, better, more alive than I have the whole of my life. I feel that I have worked for this, to integrate. We are all called to integrate our unique capacities for creativity, action, and living.

Life took me in the directions of psychotherapy and yoga. I knew R. D. Laing quite well at the time when he was giving inspiring seminars, and some of these happened to be around the topic of intra-uterine life and the beginning of life. I was pregnant around the same time and wanted my baby to have a great intra-uterine life. I believe this is the basis for health, health in general—emotional, psychological, and physical. The beginning of life is where our blueprints are laid down for the rest.

That path I have taken; the coincidence of being pregnant, doing yoga, and studying the anatomy and physiology of how women's bodies work, these were the shoots that have become the inspiration for my life and work with pregnant women.

I always believed we must be designed by nature to give birth efficiently like all the other mammals. But, somehow, the way culture imprinted on birth in recent centuries is to increasingly look at birth as a medical procedure that women cannot do by themselves. Somehow, by hospitalising most births, women are encouraged to feel that they are at risk giving birth to a baby. The surveillance around pregnancy focuses on problems and attempts to identify problems, which does not do much to instil confidence in a woman that her body is performing perfectly well.

Somebody once said that fear is the enemy of the birthing room, and I concur. A lot of pregnant women are afraid, some of them are even afraid of the baby growing inside, of becoming mothers, of their own ability to have a baby who is normal, of their capacity to love. There are so many fears, including the possibility that something might go wrong. The epidemic of fear characterises our culture; we are driven by it in so many ways, because we have lost connectivity with faith in ourselves as living beings—and as organisms, in some way. Yet there is a massive positive change taking place; on the whole we are becoming more in touch and less fearful.

I have tried to provide a space for taking care of our pregnant women without inducing unnecessary fear, helping them gain confidence in their body's abilities to make a baby, to carry a baby, to birth a baby, and to nurture a baby. These are normal inherited capacities in a woman. We need to help her find that, so she may tap into this realm beyond fear.

How do you transform fear-based experiences into the ability to celebrate the life-force within us? It is basically through exploration, through awareness, and via the body. It was my own experience of doing yoga while being pregnant that brought forth awareness of that deep transformational connection the two of these experiences had to offer. I found it very empowering to gather pregnant women together and through the vehicle of yoga we connected, they connected with each other and their unborn babies. Yoga is helpful but it is but a vehicle for gathering. By getting together and spending time together we become a tribe, circles where other women are going through similar and incredible life changes, where they enter a new phase of their lives, of the life cycle. It is this shared meeting in itself that brings about a change, one that allows the women to feel safer in sharing their emotional transformation.

Giving birth is a very animalistic thing to do; it is not a civilised thing to do. Active birth yoga (Balaskas, 1983) helps women in practicing positions and movements that are normal for birth—standing, kneeling, moving in certain ways, making certain sounds, I help them rehearse what I have seen women do instinctively, and they can therefore connect with what I call a birthing-body. What characterises a birthing-body is a woman who carries her baby with dignity, elegance, and pride. The freedom of the body to move, to choose positions that feel comfortable and productive is the very first principle of active birth (Balaskas, 1983) and women know how to find it all by themselves. Naturally, the freedom to move is necessary in other areas of our lives—and we need to experience ourselves as physical bodies every single day.

Over the years I found that the pregnant body is amazing to work with because hormonally everything is softening and there is a surrender of a kind and yielding into the body, which makes it easy to take women there. They appreciate learning to be gentle, and by that they learn to inhabit and love their body anew. What women find is not from someone else, even though I am a motherly guide, what they find is really that which is inherent inside them. Pregnant women belong to an ancient culture of birthing and that is not very difficult to connect with. All you need to do is start going into positions like all fours and dropping the head, without attempting to control everything, and by becoming responsive to what actually is happening—allowing the body to lead. And they can connect with this; I honestly do not know how but they do it. The knowledge of giving birth is genetically programmed into us as it is into all mammals, and I simply try to help women get in touch with their animal nature.

Nature has not designed a birthing process to be so painful that women would not want to go through it. It would not be a very successful model. Other mammals do not usually scream in pain when they are giving birth. Certainly, there can be problems with animals too but they do not scream in pain. Instead, they tend to look very surrendered. For me, the practice of surrender is something I aspire to do daily. Waking up in the morning, the first thing I do (after having something to drink) is get on my yoga mat, and practises a series of different postures, and at the end doing half an hour of simply sitting with awareness and focus on my breathing. In fact, it is not doing anything for half an hour, just letting myself be with myself and with whatever else comes to me during that time. This is a rich time for insights and perspective. There is something crucially important in having a little bit of time each day for simply being with our physical body. For me, there has to be some kind of self-love in it, because you are celebrating; this is a constant reminder of being a physical body. I find that the release that comes with yoga postures followed by time with myself is really useful as a practice of surrender. When we are sufficiently relaxed into our bodies we are able to perceive the presence of energy that is there at all times. I do not believe that you can seriously tune into this incredible energetic body if you are not tuned to your own body, which is where the heart of practice is.

Working with pregnant women, and sometimes with couples too, especially when we are working through touch and body experiences, I sense—and so do they—a sort of feeling of peace that seems to descend into the room. I feel it too in meditation, in my own yoga practice. We may call it divinity of some sort. I take women and couples into little journeys that are the essence of what being pregnant is all about. And then somehow, by going into these experiences in such a bodily, informal, and supportive way, they become happy, confident, and connected to this energetic body of theirs.

Of course there are the other sides to it—the shadow of the body that holds depression, aggression, fear. We all have them, and it is preciously important to be familiar with them. For many years I have been working through the darker parts of my consciousness, and it had become a disciplined practice for me, liberating me to be present, to be in touch with the deeper aspects of my being. If I feel depressed I go into it, just letting it manifest, noticing my energy go, I notice myself run out of my body . . . I notice all these things, I notice I have gone to what I call fear mode. When something does not shift by itself I seek help, but when it does, it works its way through until this presence, this divinity, comes back. I do not believe we can be in touch with our bodies if we are not connecting with the earth beneath us, the air that surrounds us, and engaging in that is miraculous—that is when divinity shows up. We are creatures of the earth, and when we lose our connection with our earth qualities, it is a little bit like not being in touch with the dark side of your psyche. And we need our earth. You cannot have heaven without earth.

I see life as a continual process of evolving and transformation, and the transformation is to come from within; the dark side of ourselves is where the key to surrender lies.

These are my personal beliefs, in the darkness inside there is always a key. If you can go into a dark place, and keep breathing, and hold your own, and see what you feel inside, my experience is that divinity comes in. Then it feels like something that was locked is now opened, and then I am like that for a while, until I get drawn into the dark place again. This is what living is—going deep inside, finding truths, and then being released from whatever it is you do to resist. We need to work through terror for that. As a post-holocaust generation Jewish woman, many things happened in my life and there was everything there for me to get completely frozen by terror, but terror has been my key to surrender, and then to divinity.

I have always been searching for something, for truth and meaning, and for faith. I went through life, studying psychology, Buddhism, yoga; looking for something . . . and I am just beginning to realise fully that what I was looking for was a way to feel connected with what people call God, divinity, it always seemed to me to be the most important thing in life. When I was pregnant I found it almost came naturally, since pregnancy involves being part of this amazing renewal, new life on this planet. The same thing that makes flowers bloom and fruits fall from the trees is now happening in your own body. In that sense pregnancy is such a gift. To have an actual baby growing in your body is a very great help to feel part of the miracle of life.

Learning to enter into your vital body, to get to know yourself as the person you are; the vital body, the vital mind, the vital entirety that you are, is a lifetime journey, and it is the best thing you can do with your life. It is through that you learn to love yourself, to love other people, and to contribute, in your work, to a better world.

CHAPTER FIVE

Dialogue: the living body

Janet Balaskas, Silke Ziehl, Asaf Rolef Ben-Shahar, Liron Lipkies, and Noa Oster

ilke Ziehl: Reading your piece, Janet, I notice that when working with birth and around birth, you communicate with mother and baby at the same time, holding both of them in awareness. I loved your explicitness about spirituality because I never quite dared to be that explicit.

Janet Balaskas: I have spent thirty years with groups of pregnant mothers and their babies and sometimes the fathers too. And often, when I am teaching, and there might be fifteen babies there, there is a kind of energy present which cannot be denied, and I think this is because of the presence of unborn babies. They are the purest form of our living body.

Editors: You both speak of awareness and make a connection between awareness and aliveness. Could you expand on that? Somehow it seems that aliveness is invited through awareness, would you say something about that?

SZ: As you ask I notice my whole body responding. For me that response is part of awareness, but there is a step beyond that is like a spark. Aliveness for me is in that spark in-between, the spark that connects. It's not in my head; it's what happens in the space between that involves a meeting. It's something that really jumps out when we share something, whether verbally or nonverbally. Oddly, like a baby who cannot yet talk but I can pick him up or not—I could ignore him—and there is something which happens when we communicate, when that spark, which includes a sense of me and you from both directions, emerges.

JB: For me, the first thing I became aware of when you asked the question was my own heart beating, and what my eyes could see as I looked at you. Awareness is multisensory as well as mental. It is to do with what you think as well, and it involves perception on many levels. I agree with Silke about relatedness but for me, awareness comes from the feeling of yourself. It is from the internal that you perceive the external. Awareness is an amazing capacity that humans share, and many animals have it too.

SZ: *The Secret Life of Plants* (Tompkins & Bird, 1989) suggests that plants have awareness too and they stay connected with the people they are familiar with, and recognise and respond to what happens to those people. The connection with my cat helps me remember myself; I call my cat when I reach London and say "come on, I am coming". Sometimes I have a sense of linking in with plants at home. Thinking out loud, perhaps awareness relates to the life force in all things that are organic, something around the ability to link.[1]

Eds: So perhaps awareness is not something that we have but something that we might partake in, or tap into. In your paper, Janet, you speak of allowing women to connect to their birthing body, it's as if there is a birthing body that is imminent in them and they just need to tap into.

JB: Yes, it is about being in harmony with something bigger than ourselves that we are part of.

SZ: I can at times shut my awareness down, and be completely oblivious of anybody or anything around me, and sometimes I do it through choice while at other times I slide into it. I can also be disconnected. Doing it consciously I call it opening or closing the gate, and feel it's important for me to open and close my gate depending on what is my ability, and where I am, and what I want to do at the time. For example, when I start working with somebody, I will open my boundaries and let the client enter, and then the session is finished I close the gate again.

JB: To some extent, we have some control of our awareness. And we can focus our awareness as well. For example, when a woman goes through labour, the great art of being able to give birth is the ability to focus her awareness within and with what is happening and she can shut down her awareness to everything else. So we can play with awareness.

Eds: It seems that there are times where we are at liberty to play with our awareness, and other times where we feel frozen and lacking of control. In both your pieces, there seems to be a continuous link between aliveness and terror, body aliveness and body terror. Can you say more about that?

SZ: I was attempting to show that there is hope for life—even for an organism who has been so completely terrorised, who soaked up terror and pain in such an intense form. But he could recover the ability to welcome life, to welcome unpredictability and surprises so that he could learn that there was a landscape beyond terror again.

His whole bodymind has a sense of life; there is okayness in life which was not there initially. And now this mischievous little boy is very alive and in his own body in a funny kind of way. I too am a fearful person, and I've been through the frightening times; something in me knows about daring to be alive because I've survived. Life is about risk, it's about daring to invite the unexpected, because if it is all predictable it's not alive. What do you think, Janet?

JB: Personally, for me terror has been an avenue of growth. In my youth I was so terrified that my awareness was quite limited, my ability to let in love or give love was in some sense frozen. I lost my mother when I was nine-years-old and various things happened that led me to be terrified, although I think we all have terror and anxieties that are part of who we are. Eventually, I went into psychotherapy which has been a very long journey of transformation and the most recent work I have done is to acknowledge and express terror and fear because it has a way to evaporating when I do. Fear is very constricting and isolating but if you really experience that isolation and constriction, terror seems to certainly dissipate, at least until the next time you are in that place. You get tools to work through that quicker and it had taken me quite a while. Today I can mostly distinguish between myself and the terrified constricted state, and have tools to express and release it.

SZ: Funny, because as you were talking my hand was reaching out because I sometimes reach out in my imagination to somebody else there, not necessarily in reality. But I need to have a voice in the ear— I need another human being in order to face terror.

JB: I think that's true.

SZ: I can do it with somebody else, and invite or be invited to go to my own terror with somebody who's exploring that. Because for me the root of terror is helplessness and aloneness, that's my worst fantasy.

JB: I don't really need to physically be with another person, but I do need a link to someone if I get overwhelmed by terror. Even now, as we speak, I recognise the bodily sensation of terror; that pit in my stomach, the raise of the heartbeat, circular movements of the mind. It's very unpleasant when our mind does these circular erratic move-ments, basically going nowhere. And if I can bring myself back into my body and feel the sensations of terror with curious experiential enquiry, and be there and breathe and use techniques I've learned to flow with that awareness, then it dissolves. Then comes love, grati-tude, peace, and that is both my own work with myself, and what I do with the women I see.

Eds: You leave us wondering whether people who are fighting for life could be so adamant without having known their unalive or dead parts; since both of you have very strong dead parts from which you move into aliveness.

JB: Not knowing our darkness is dangerous. We would be in a safer world if all people could extend their awareness to those aspects of themselves. If these are not felt, known or safely expressed it's much easier for one to act them out and be harmful to self and others, and a lot of what is going on in our planet is exactly that syndrome.

Eds: So, how do you go through the unaware or the hard-to-call-forth states?

SZ: Two things are important for me here. Firstly, I can only do it when my arms metaphorically stretch out with a sense of including the unaware parts as a part of me. Secondly, by not fighting with them. If I start fighting against these parts it becomes a struggle, and one of us must lose. But when I have that sense physically in my body, it's almost like I assume from the beginning it is there, and when I can hold that knowledge that aliveness is there and that I include all the parts that are there, then somehow the spark can grow. It cannot grow if I struggle with parts of me or with the other and if there is an expectation to "get there" or "to relax". But if I can let go of that sense, of struggle or having to achieve something, and note that it is already there, it tends to shows itself.

JB: I am not sure how I do it. Perhaps recognising that all feelings are there to start with, and coming to it organically. When I meet a pregnant woman, we debate, I meet her husband; I offer them a whole variety of different things. There is a yoga class, and we are being together in a circle. Sometimes I feel that I've done it very well and at other times I am disappointed with myself, I think that's the nature of the work. And I would like to further develop these capacities. How I see myself moving in the future is perhaps deepening the work with pregnant women, so that we can explore, assist them in being connected with their birthing body, and like you said Silke, it is there. It is actually there and it is like calling forth and many people find it, but to different degrees. I am very lucky working with pregnant women because I've got nature on my side; all the hormones naturally softening the tendency towards healing and health, and all I need is to provide the space for that to happen.

SZ: For me, it's about daring. If I don't dare to put myself into the situation fully I never reach the other fully. The deepening is daring for me, daring to be a bit more, showing myself a bit more, since naturally I am a very shy person.

JB: Oddly, I would say the same of myself; I make a lot of noise for a shy person. I am inherently quite shy.

Eds: But you do more than providing space. You both hold a horizon. You, Janet, are talking about birthing body and knowing it is there; you are holding in your bodymind and assuming it's already there. The women simply have to follow but you're already holding it. And you, Silke, are talking about knowing there is an aliveness there, and there is something about holding faith in the goodness and not just looking at what is not working.

SZ: I am not interested in only discovering what is not working. I am really interested in seeing the spark of life come out, it's not about cleaning the oven, but about making a fire.

JB: Faith that a woman can give birth and that the baby knows how to be born, underlies everything I do. I'm not denying that complications can occur, but I feel there is no point in focusing on anxiety and fear of complications. We do much better to focus on larger possibilities, that women know how to give birth, that their body, their mind, their heart, and soul know how to give birth, and that babies know exactly how and when to be born. We don't need all these external anxieties that the system puts on the birthing mother and the baby. The faith that I hold is neither uneducated nor blind faith. I have a deep knowing of this faith; it's not flimsy in any way. I am absolutely sure about it. I cannot tell how I do it in terms of methodology, but I could give you a few clues, practical ideas and clues. I feel I am lucky enough to manage to discover what and how I manage to contribute with my professional life and all the experiences I've had in my life. I have gained faith through having four children, through giving birth four times. The work I have done on myself and everything I have learned from my life experience helped building up this faith. And I found a way to pass that on to others, which is quite often beneficial for them, and I wish to keep honouring that in myself with learning and growing further. Faith is where the heart of it all is for me.

SZ: Listening to you and reflecting, I think what first came up is that I felt I have been encouraged to cultivate awareness, most explicitly through my training in Hawaiian Shamanism. The sense of interconnectedness with everything and everybody around, and the responsibility to myself and to all around me that I learned from that training, these taught me to cultivate awareness. I have also held not a religious belief, because that never resonated with me, but a sense of connectedness, even had as a child. I felt it as I needed to make connection with the trees, the sky, and life around in order to be able to breathe. And that stayed with me later on as well. It makes sense in terms of the whole notion of the Chinese worldview (Connelly, 1994), which felt so right for me when I trained in Chinese medicine. Chinese philosophy holds what is important for me and that worldview concerns a sense of connectedness not only to people but to the world as a living organism, the seasons, and time. For me, it is a physical sensation, it's an opening of sorts, allowing myself to open up to a wider reality. For example, in supervision I often ask "what do you think is the larger context to that person?" This is very important, because if you get lost in the small details of daily life you may lose sight that this soul has chosen a particular kind of experience. I have nothing to base my belief on except trust that we choose to come here to do something, to experience something; that there is a larger context of everybody's existence. At the darkest and most desperate times, it's useful to remember that it's about a choice; that people have come down here and they want to take something from being here and from being alive—this is an integral part of what I try to remember and convey.

JB: As you were speaking, Silke, I was wondering where is this source of what we do? I think that my biggest trauma was losing my mother at nine, and now I have ended up being somebody who helps hundreds of women to become mothers, and to find connection with their babies—a connection that I myself lost. In a way, when life provides you with your most painful, traumatic, difficult things, it also holds a key if you are lucky or willing to explore that, assisting you in becoming whole again and giving back.

SZ: For me, it is such a privilege to be alive. I am kind of grateful for all these experiences and meetings and connections and all the things I have been able to play with and do in this life.

Eds: Speaking of doing, what kind of practices do you cultivate to keep you alive?

SZ: I am talking with or stroking my cat; I am looking at the sky, and letting the world go by. This is really important. There is something about the silly everyday experiences that is important. I can of course do Qi Gong, but it's my cat that reminds me of life most. If I am really lost I imagine stroking my cat. It's like . . . that's my emergency connection.

Eds: Perhaps this is one of the places where you are slightly different from each other. Silke keeps emphasising interpersonal and intersubjective connections, the need of the other, and Janet, in choosing to be a midwife, continuously emphasises the intrapsychic connection, the connection inside and the spiritual connection. And we notice the aliveness you mention is thus slightly different.

JB: We are different, of course. For me, the strongest connection comes through silence and stillness. I find the attention to my breathing and surrender to the earth really important. I lie on my back every day with my knees bent and I close my eyes and let my body go and pay attention to my breathing, and then sit for a few minutes in silence each day. These are the times when I get it. Certainly, it could also be going for a walk in nature, but breathing is always there for me.

Eds: It's fascinating how we each draw our aliveness from different sources.

JB: I suppose I am also going through a period of my life of being quite a lot alone and I have discovered how to enjoy being alone, so I am not so focused on the other at the moment. It's just how it is. I am very pleased to have met you, Silke, and feel curious and interested in the person you are.

SZ: I was just thinking how amazing that you brought us together because there is such a lot of overlaps and I can breathe in your presence and I don't have to worry.

Note

1.   This view is on a par with Gregory Bateson's (1979) understanding of mind as a dialectic process shared by all organic matter [Editors].

PART III

THE SENSUAL BODY

Introduction to Part III

What do we want to let into our bodies? What do we want to push out? Sex and food, our main channels for choosing what enters our physical body (and what is rejected), both speak the language of sensuality and passion. Such choices involve strong emotions, and through the history of humanity and psychotherapy within it we have been preoccupied with both food and sex. Hence, we wanted both here, in this section.

Sexuality and passion are powerful forces. Whether we look at sex through drive-theory or through relational conceptualisations, eroticism impacts us forcefully—it impacts our choices and our behaviours, our values and the course of our lives; it impacts individuals, and it impacts cultures and societies. Psychoanalyst Sabina Spielrein (1912) described the sex drive as holding potential for aliveness and death, surrender and fears of annihilation, destruction and creativity.

Working with eroticism in psychotherapy therefore holds these potentials and risks, explosiveness and vitality, at its very core. Body psychotherapist Shoshi Asheri (2004) boldly wrote: "I believe that engaging with the erotic is a key for therapeutic transformation. I believe the erotic provokes and excites growth. It is an expression of the desire for connection and integration." And the bodily aspects of sensuality and sexuality cannot be denied.

To explore the interweaving pulse between bodies, therapy, sensuality, and passion we have invited two very special writers. Psychotherapist and author Esther Perel is one of the most widely known experts on working with eroticism, and she brings a wealth of knowledge, curiosity, inspiration, and integration into her writing. Alongside her we can find Master Chef Eyal Shani, one of the leading culinary mavericks in Israel and a man who looks at the world through eyes of sensuality and passion. Following their individual pieces, Esther and Eyal embark (over a glass of wine) on a passionate discussion on intimacy, life choices, storytelling, and sensuality.

You are invited to loosen your body and join this delicious exploration.

CHAPTER SIX

In search of erotic intelligence*

Esther Perel

Sustaining desire in the long haul requires the reconciliation of two opposing human needs: our need for security and stability, and our quest for passion and adventure. These two opposing forces of freedom and commitment are difficult to merge in modern marriage. On the one hand, we seek a steady and reliable anchor in our partner. On the other, we expect love to offer transcendent experiences, allowing us to soar beyond the mundane and ordinary. How do we reconcile the need for safety with the wish for excitement, mystery, and fire? This challenge is not merely psychological or practical; it is also a systemic one. This paper will highlight some key principles that guide my therapeutic work with individuals and couples who seek to cultivate lasting erotic intimacy.

The language of the body (sex comes first)

Our earliest interactions with our environment and our carers are dominated by bodily sensations. The body serves as a memory bank

---

*Edited by Danit Rachmilevitz, with thanks.

of our sensual pleasures of the skin, in infancy and throughout our lives. Our entire emotional history plays itself out in the physicality of sex. The body is the purest, most primal vessel we have for communication.

Yet the body does not only hold the history of our pleasure, it also stores the distress and frustration we have endured through life, the pain we have suffered. Our bodies intelligently remember what our minds have chosen to forget, both pleasure and pain, light and dark.

Traditional psychotherapy tends to leave the body out of the conversation. When focus does shift to the body, it is mostly with the focus on pain. Indeed, this permits exploring experiences of traumas and how these are stored in the body. Sex too is mostly investigated through lenses of pain, hurt, abuse, and shame. However, the body in bliss, sexual connection, and pleasure is too often left out. The wisdom of the healing body is not fully explored, and neither are the invitation, the surrender, and the ecstasy of melting bodies.

Therapists are frequently reluctant to ask about sex and often hope that the client will never bring it up. What exactly prevents them from bringing up sexuality? Is it the concern about making clients feel uncomfortable? A fear that introducing sexuality might be overstepping the clients' boundaries? But are we not intrusive when we probe the depths of our client's emotional life? Arlene Lev and Jean Malpas (2011) ask if by probing into clients' lives and at the same time avoiding sexuality, we are not unwittingly participating in "the social condoning of emotional pornography, expecting clients to expose the deepest details of their personal history, while sanctioning sexuality as private and taboo?"(p. 4).

The typical therapeutic premise is that sexual problems always result from troubled relationships. Hence we should focus on improving the relationships first and upon that sex will follow. But, my experience suggests otherwise. I helped many couples to improve their relationships but their sex life remained the same. They felt closer, less conflictual, laughing more, and feeling more complicitous, but what helped in the kitchen did not necessarily do much for the bedroom. Talking about relationships without talking about sex perpetuates the avoidant behaviour.

In my teaching and practice, I invert the therapeutic priorities and ask about the partners' sexuality first. Sexuality becomes the window into the self, a portal into the couple's dynamics and their families of origin. Sex is not a metaphor for the relationships, but rather a parallel narrative, one that speaks its own language and is addressed directly.

The body has its own language and its own vocabulary; it is a vital language—the universal mother tongue. As a therapist, I teach my clients to be bilingual. They are taught to listen, to understand, and to experience the language of their body. I teach them to speak the language of touch, and use touch in many forms in the therapy room. Touch is indeed an intricate matter, and working with it depends on the client and the context of therapy. With some clients it is only natural to use touch, while with others it is foreign. I have trained couples to exercise with their partner different forms of touch such as "touch me without touching", becoming accustomed to energetic touch. They learn the difference between giving touch, taking touch, healing touch, erotic touch, sensual touch, and so forth. I try to speak with my clients at least three languages at all times: the languages of feeling, thinking, and sensing. It entails observing the clients' body language. How people embody themselves, how they breathe, how they respond to touch and movement. And as we learn to speak more fluent body, our relationships alter: frequently, when our experience of the body and our sexuality changes, everything else in the relationship changes too.

Erotic intimacy

The relationship between intimacy and sexuality is complex and therapists have long tried to elucidate the Gordian knot of intimacy and sexuality. Emotional intimacy and talk intimacy are not the same as erotic intimacy, which deserves and needs to be addressed separately, and worked with directly in order to create change. Eroticism is the quality of aliveness, of vibrancy and vitality that extends way beyond the biology of sex or the sexual repertoire of techniques. It captures our longing for radiance and transcendence.

My focus on eroticism comes from my work with traumatised populations and from growing up in Holocaust survivors' community. My parents were holocaust survivors and I, characteristically, lived life as a counter-phobic. This inheritance from the Holocaust meant that while I had many fears, I insisted on not letting them consume me, knowing that everything might vanish in a moment. Similarly, in my community, I observed two groups: those who did not die and those who came back to live. For those who did not die, pleasure was tainted by feelings of guilt and fear. Those who came back to life were eager to re-enter the world, to reconnect with their playfulness and pleasure—to take risks. These people tend to experience the erotic as an antidote to death.

As a second generation to Holocaust survivors, I experienced the split between those two parts personally. As a young adult I used to oscillate between feeling melancholy and vibrancy. While experiencing the dark part I thought that was the only truth and when I was in the lively joyous part I could not remember the feeling and the despair of the other part. It took me many years to integrate those two aspects, and my intention is to reconcile this split between pain and joy, deadness and aliveness, feeling and sensing in my work with students, with clients and in my life.

Seeking this integration brought me to explore eroticism as a form of play. Eroticism is the cultivation of excitement, a purposeful cultivation of pleasure for its own sake. Sex often remains the last arena of play we allow ourselves to partake in, a bridge to our childhood. Long after the mind has been indoctrinated to be serious, the body longs to return to the playground, free from inhibition, fear, and judgment.

Erotic intimacy holds a tension between the various parts of who we are. It captures how we reveal core aspects of ourselves through the language of sex: our wishes, our dreams, our aspirations, our fears, and our challenges. Erotic intimacy is a unique form of intimacy. The erotic landscape is vastly larger, richer, and more intricate than the proliferation of sexual acts. Sex is a replicate of our longing, our fears, and struggles, and we therefore invest our erotic encounters with preliminary sets of needs and expectations. We seek love, pleasure, escape, ecstasy. We wish to be seen and we even aspire to find spiritual union.

People and therapists tend to relate to sex as something we do. Couples often come to therapy with their "doing sex" story of acts, techniques, and statistics. However, sex is not something we do; it is a place where we go inside ourselves and with another, or others. Couples need help in entering their subjective and intersubjective experience. In therapy, we explore the role of sex in the couple's life: What does sex mean to you? What do you seek in sex? What do you want to experience in your erotic encounters? Is it connection; surrender; a safe space for aggression, a temporary loss of self, as in flow? Naughtiness, boundary permutation? How do you experience conflicts around pleasure? How do you see yourself being seen? Many of those questions are tied in with cultural messages, expressed in the body, and these too need to be unpacked.

The central agent of eroticism is our imagination, or in the words of Proust (2002): "The only real journey, the only Fountain of Youth, would be to travel not towards new landscapes, but with new eyes" (p. 237). Eroticism is not focused on new sexual positions. Instead we continue to cultivate our new eyes, developing our imagination, approaching our partner with compelling curiosity, and at the same time remain interesting and attractive to ourselves and to another.

The challenge in sexual therapy and couple therapy is in cultivating eroticism, in the sense of having pleasurable relationships with our vitality and with our openness. We ought to explore more than our pain. This is a central point in my work, since focusing on marital and sexual problems without also exploring the pleasures therein is partial and ineffective. How can one have better sex by only talking about not wanting sex? Sex is a quintessential bodily mediated experience. The joy of the body and the joy of sexual encounters are bizarrely absent from many people's lives, and when this is also absent from psychotherapy it perpetuates the same systematic problem.

The archaeology of desire

The psychology of desire can often be found buried in the details of our childhood. By digging through our early history, we can uncover its archaeology. Our emotional history shapes our erotic blueprints, and is thereafter expressed in the physicality of sex.

Sex therapist Jack Morin (1995) argues that erotic imagination is inventive in undoing, transforming, and re-addressing the traumas of the past. That is, the very experiences that have caused the most pain in our childhood stand a chance of becoming a source of pleasure and excitement later on in our lives. Here lays the mystery of eroticism, love, and desire—they relate in conflict, dialectically shaping each other.

The challenge of sexual intimacy is therefore in reclaiming and bringing home the erotic. It is the most intimidating of intimacies because it is all-encompassing. Erotic intimacy reaches the deepest places within us, requiring us to disclose aspects of ourselves to another that are invariably bound up with shame and guilt. It is frightening, and in erotic intimacy we are found manifesting a whole new kind of nakedness, far more revealing than the sight of our nude bodies. In expressing our erotic yearnings, we dare to risk humiliation and rejection, both carrying a highly devastating prospect (Perel, 2007).

Our attitudes to sex and intimacy are shaped by our past. We have learned to relate to our body, our gender, and our sexuality from our carers' responses to our needs. Tell me how you were loved, and I will tell you how you make love. I attempt to learn about the massages that couples and individuals have accumulated and internalised, about issues of autonomy and freedom, connection and dependency. These messages will shape their ability to manage the dialectic relationship between love and desire.

For example, think of two children sitting on their mothers' lap. At some point, they wish to jump off and run, exploring their world. They are attentive to the cues from the adult they have just left. One may say, "Go ahead, the world is a beautiful place to explore." The second mother might respond differently, with fear and anxiety. Those massages will define an opposite attachment pattern. The first child would experience freedom and connection, and will be able to sense both the security of love and the autonomy of desire. As an adult, this will turn into playful eroticism, with the capacity to alternate between the danger of hiding and seeking and the relief of being found. The second child will have fewer options. He might remain with the parent, in order not to lose connection, thus giving up a part of himself. Growing up, he might have a hard time making love with the people he loves. Worrying and taking responsibility for the person he loves could shut off the spontaneity and selfness necessary for erotic abandon. The self-absorption inherent in sexual excitement would be perceived as obliterating the other in a way that collides with the ideal of intimacy (Perel, 2010). The person might remain stuck. Therapy is therefore also about re-imprinting.

Let me illustrate with a case example. In working with a couple, it transpired that the man has never touched his partner's face in the twenty-six years they have been together. Holding someone's face in your hands can create an ultimate non-threatening focus between the two. Asking the man to touch his partner's face, I left the room to give them space. While I was outside, I realised that he was asked to do something he had no idea how to approach. Trying it for the second time, I asked the couple whether they would like me to stay or step out. Both of them asked me to stay. The woman held the man like a boy. I had to help her move back, so that they may shift between the needing of a mother to wanting her as a woman. They needed help in differentiating motherly touch from sexual touch. Both needs are valid, but the confusion between the parental and the sexual is erotically fatal, retrieving distinction was an important first step.

Desire needs novelty, mystery, otherness, and differentness. It seeks to go where it has not been before. On the other hand, love needs stability, harmony, and understanding, wishing to contrast and bridge distance. Erotic intimacy is the dialectic tension, the ambiguous space between anxiety and fascination.

CHAPTER SEVEN

La petite mort

Master Chef Eyal Shani

Wanting nothing in return

Jerusalem. Two floors above my house resides Congo's embassy.

As a five-year-old I loved collecting stamps, and took pleasure in the moments where I laid my hands on rare stamps. To my great delight, the embassy of Congo above provided me with many such moments of pleasure. They used to receive letters with big stamps on them, of cheetahs, rhinos, and other wild animals, the coolest stamps there were. At the time there was no diplomatic mail or paper shredders, and the envelopes were all thrown into the garbage; naivety.

The workers in the embassy were black, and I remember their beautiful colour so different to my skin and the skin of their secretary, which was snow-white, and was made even whiter in contrast with theirs. Once a day, usually at the same time, she went down to the garbage bin to empty the trash, where the big envelopes resided as treasures hiding my desired stamps. And so these precious moments became a ritual for me. I would reach the pavement, climb the low fence, overlooking the garbage bin, and waiting. The secretary was perhaps in her thirties, she had large breasts forever covered in a smart white shirt with one too many undone buttons. I would stand there, looking at her breasts as she bent over to empty the trash. And then, in that moment, something extraordinary happened, she always did bend and for a fragment of a second remain there longer than she needed to; as if she had done it for me. I wondered why she did it, and I came to the conclusion it was the generosity of her heart. Surely she wanted nothing of this five year old, I knew she wanted nothing from me. She did it because she realised I was enjoying her and was secretly prepared to give me something for nothing, wanting nothing in return.

In my sexual experience, I always desire giving something for nothing, something beyond my interests and desires, which will emerge from this very purity of giving and wanting nothing in return. This is of my essence. This woman bestowed this gift upon me. This woman, who was willing to spare a second for me. Like musical timing, waiting. Waiting, which includes everything within it. And generosity. When these elements are found in sex, then it remains pure and rich of emotions.

The liquid laws of the state

Sexuality is not a place of hierarchy, but a meeting. In a certain moment I am meeting the other and a circle is created between us, and we resonate one another; like birth, fertilisation between male and female. Something new is created, something primal that has immense power since it is non-replicable, and therefore fully alive, made of newly breathing cells and not from previously known ones. This is what my encounter with food looks like.

I know that in order to make food I need to understand how to build a skyscraper, how a leaf lives its life, and learn the hidden land-scape of the roots of a tree, since if I do not know these things, I would not know how to cook. I do not receive information about food from the food itself, because then at best I will learn to cook the food but fail to understand its desires, its wishes. To comprehend these desires and aspirations I observe food as someone and not as something, I meet with him or her.

This meeting oscillates between the intimate and the non-intimate. Intimacy is the space between two bodies, two souls, between feelings, and as long as this space exists—so does intimacy. But as soon as these bodies merge intimacy disappears and a one is created. The one is not intimacy, it is fusion.

When I am facing a cucumber I want to become it, to know it from inside, I want to get to know it, its magma, everything that it is. Its beauty and the perfection embedded within it, compels me to enter it. When I cook a cucumber I make love to it in the most basic form, I penetrate it. This thing called a cucumber is amorphous, it is not a vegetable in terms of the speed of its development, yet just as speedily it becomes meaningless and dies so shortly after you disconnect it from its bush. To fuse with a cucumber I need to understand that the cucumber deals with fluid-discipline. It is like a state with its own liquid laws. It tastes ever so weak, scarcely anybody cooks with it, and those who try would find that as soon as you put it in a dish, its liquid-tensions rapidly change, the mineral quality changes, and even the electrical conductivity changes. This cucumber has such immense powers, it is the holder of deep knowledge about organising water and liquid, and this is where its uniqueness lies.

As soon as I become this cucumber, a fusion takes place, and I can, as if I was channelling it, read it and cook its qualities. I do not know a different way. I cannot withstand being outside of the cucumber. Everybody in the world lives outside of it, knowing how lovely it is to cut it and, together with a piece of cheese, put it on a slice of bread. I cannot be that person, nor am I interested in being like this. I approach the cucumber from a zero point, a point where I do not know how to cook. Not knowing is my natural state of being, this is the zero, this is how I trained myself to remember nothing. If I remember, my powers of creation will weaken and I would need to recycle, and if I would need to recycle I would wish to die, this is too difficult to tolerate.

The place where water yearns for itself

When I engage in creativity, I make a medium, a vessel for realising myself. Another person may choose to be dancer, another a sculptor, a hairdresser, or a cook. The material is secondary. The material is the binder. When I fill a cup with water, I can fill it so that the water touches slightly above the rim, this is pretty amazing. It happens because internal tension is created. The water gathers inwardly, eager to itself, yearning for itself. This is sexuality. As soon as the water would cross this threshold of internal tension it would spill, no more sexuality, no more passion.

Passion is the place where the water yearns for itself, knows itself. Knowing yourself is sexy and this is where the beginning of sexuality relates to identity definition. Where do I stand? What is mine and what is the other's? Where do I belong and what is my direction? A person needs to be complete and homogenous to be desired, to know his or her own body cells, and allow the messages that seeps through his or her skin to sing and tell their story.

Fertilisation

When I touch food, when I cook—the whole world disappears and the food becomes my whole world; this is complete totality. Thanks to it I manage to connect with my inner clockwork where I have an opportunity to make adjustments. I might send a virtual vehicle into the person, loaded up it is sent inside—this is what I do with food, it is a vehicle. At my best, when I fine-tune my watches I can charge them up with energy and introduce them into the body of the other, and as long as these energies are benevolent I can perform miracles with the person who ingests my food. Another possibility is for me to fuse, to join the other body and become it for a certain immeasurable time, to fully become one with the other. During that time I fine-tune and make slight adjustments. Something happens that cannot take place without surrender to fusion. I do not create hierarchy—that is, there is no judgment here concerning good or bad, high or low, beautiful or ugly. Instead, the meeting is the dissolving of all known materials, feelings, sensations, bodies, forces—all is activated during that moment.

This is what I do with each person who comes to eat with me. Saying it bluntly, when someone comes to me I am supposed to stun him and trap him. I am aware that I have to unmake his familiar boundaries, for he arrives with old boundaries and blocks through which he understands his narrative. But this is not my culinary narrative, for him to partake in my culinary narrative he needs to surrender and understand that the rules are different here, even though he is well familiar with them. I do not take him to Mars, no, I leave him in his own home; right here. I serve him with an array of tastes that he knows all too well, only changing the combination . . . this is where the explosion occurs, this is when I shall penetrate him with all those charged energies.

This is passion at it rawest form, passion wishing to surrender you and fertilise you; a missionary conquest of sorts. This is how I lead my life, this is everything I have. Food is my way of entering people and fertilising them, of having passionate sex with them.

I remember my childhood through the eyes of my grandfather, who was a significant figure in my life. He was vegan so I was brought up on cleanliness of tastes, with clear discerning, on primers rather than elaborate combinations. To this day my food is very clean in its essence. Over the years I began to understand that food was a carrier of energy and charge, bringing these into the body. I remember watching people swallow and thinking to myself—this is the deepest way to enter another person's body; it is not fucking—it is not penetration, it is fusing, dissolving into the blood, thawing. When I make food I saturate myself with the other person's blood, it is a very powerful experience. In cooking for someone I know, the mere thought of what I can give him excites and thrills me. I know what I can do to him, what I can do for him. I can tune him as I wish, I can provide him with passion, with happiness and delight, with growth and more, and I can do it without it being connected with me, but through his own body. Finally, when we part, the person will carry my own adjustments and attunement inside of him, and this grants me enormous control. It allows me to know the person in the deepest possible way; and so he is now bound to me.

I am addicted to this place, a space of conquest. And this place is about movement. I know today that the reason for my being is movement; that as long as I move I have a reason to be. There is no goal since when one gets to a goal it is realised in one second and all but disappears. Goals are so treacherous. I now understand that it is all about movement; movement comprised of conquering fragments, about the moments before; without this movement I do not know what to do and I die within seconds.

La petite mort

In French, orgasm is called *la petite mort*, meaning the little death. I can see in my mind's eyes a young French boy growing up and nearing his own *petite mort*. He is there, facing his orgasm—his little death. You need maturity to understand the meaning of it; it really is about the end. All shall end, all gone, and there is no bigger moment than this, no bigger moment than death. It means that at that particular moment I penetrate death. Sexuality, after all, includes death within it; therefore I connect with my own death. I believe that, in this respect, passion helps us get ready to die. *La petite mort*, the little death that we can tolerate, is death in smaller doses. Like in medicine, the orgasm offers the right dose of death; it is the corridor that may lead us more peacefully to the end without revolt. In orgasm there is moment of clarity; pleasure, surrendering to something bigger. In that moment I do not mind to die—I have surrendered and experienced this pleasure and I understand that the force is so huge that I am nothing in comparison to it. This self-effacement removes any fear, any struggle is futile, and the ocean can do with me as it wills. There is no fear, no regret, there is only assimilation. Death is being assimilated in this vastness. This is where sexuality resides, in the fragment of the time that the generous secretary bestowed upon me.

CHAPTER EIGHT

Dialogue: imagining desire

Esther Perel, Eyal Shani, Asaf Rolef Ben-Shahar,
Liron Lipkies, and Noa Oster

The dialogue takes place on Skype. Two countries, three bottles of wine.

Editors: We want to begin with desire and passion and people's capacity to express their desire in food and in sex. Can you say something about it?

Esther Perel: The definition of desire is to own the wanting. You can force people to eat, to have sex, and to do all kind of things, yet you can never force people to want. Wanting is a fundamental expression of freedom and sovereignty. Wanting always belongs to you. I believe that every wanting, in terms of the permission to give oneself—be it the food you want to eat, or sex, or sensuality, or connection, any wanting is ultimately predicated on a fundamental sense of self-worth. Do I deserve to want? Am I worthy enough as a person to have wants, have them expressed and to have them satisfied particularly by someone else?

Some people eat without really knowing what they want. They eat what's in front of them, or what their eye or smell caught, it's not necessarily what they really desire. We lie a lot in our relation to food, and so too in relation to our sexuality. Do we know our pleasure, can we identify it, name it, ask for it, and surrender to it? For many years when I went to restaurants I would often not order what I really wanted but rather what I thought I could afford. I would deprive myself, caught in a "ridiculous" conflict between what I thought was reasonable and what I was in the mood for. This tension between "wanting" and "should", between permission and limitation, between I want more and I have enough, can be experienced around food and around sexuality. While each of these categories has its unique features, the dance between should and wants is often very similar.

Eyal Shani: Food is an intimate space. You construct this environment, and it requires a lot of courage and time to clean the white-noise so that we may really say what we love and what we want. However, when people come to dine at my table, I refuse to address the question of what they want to eat, because I know that they cannot know what they want to eat. Even if they think they do, how can they know without having touched the food or made it? Without knowing how it was born? I need to create a reality, bridging the food that I made and experienced and them being willing to take it into their body. This is not a simple task.

We take food into our bodies, and it spreads into our bloodstream, a virus of sorts, carrying the qualities of food, and like a psychiatric drug changing the life of the person ingesting it, albeit for a limited period of time. For this change I need to tell them a story which would entice them in; to tell them a lie that would create a world: it had never been a reality. When I tell a customer what the fish experienced in the sea, it is a make-believe. I attempt to connect to the fish's movement, to its life-experience, and recreate the fish anew, telling it to the person so that he can understand that the whole world could be found in this fish, and that by consuming the fish he would ingest the whole world, receiving the soul of the world and the power therein. This is how I work.

Similarly, to bring someone to desire you is to construct a hermetic world where nothing exists except the two of you, where you are the flame of this world. It is, of course, an illusion, yet it is necessary to believe it if we wish for it to become reality. This reality can only be constructed by a dyad. This is how we cultivate passion, by telling stories and creating worlds.

EP: I completely agree with the centrality of imagination you related to, Eyal. Eroticism works through stories. My son has just asked me for a project, how I differentiate the experiences of reading a well written book from reading a badly written one. The metaphor I had was the magic trick of sawing someone in half. We all know that nobody will be sawn in half. A mediocre magician would perform the trick; it would take two minutes: someone enters the box, he cuts the box in half and there is no magic whatsoever; no sparking of imagination nor surrender into a state of suspended disbelief. But the good magician first makes all the people walking in the street, heading this way or that way stop and pay attention.. With his words he draws them in closer and closer, enticing them to look at something they have seen a thousand times before. They know exactly how it will end, but nonetheless they are willing once more to be taken into this journey, this flight of imagination.

ES: They are willing to believe. It's about enticing people to surrender, to seek nothing but the sensory pleasures of suspending disbelief. This is not a reality, but it is pleasure giving: "come and worship this pleasure alongside me for a moment," we say. Stopping the world is the most powerful force in communication today, since for us to have our words heard we need to be able to pause. Today, speed is appreciated much more than pauses. Most things become extinct because of speed. The concept of newness became an *über-concept*. Newness is the only thing that does not require us to sense into our own deep, internal void; thus we can all sense novelty and pursue it.

Eds: You both define passion as a function of storytelling, of enticing imagination that calls the other into your story. Why is the body needed as a vehicle for imagination?

EP: We need a body because we are mammals and embodied creatures, and we happen to have mind, body, and heart. We are born sensuous and we become erotic. Good lovers are not born, they are made. The central agent of eroticism is the imagination, hence we have the capacity to experience touch without being touched. We can experience the erotic, which is sexuality socialised and transformed by the human imagination. Marcel Proust said that "it is our imagination that is responsible for love, not the other person."

ES: True, the body is but a platform, a background against which we dress our imagination. The body will be enticed into imagination. Someone who is uninterested in being captivated by imagination will not go with you. I am looking for those who can come into the magical cave I create.

EP: But the body is not a magical cave for everybody. While some people experience the body as chateau where they like to linger in every room with ample time and delight, for others this home—this body—is experienced as jail and they wish nothing more than to escape it. They struggle to understand how anybody would want to enter and stay in this place that they so want to get out of. The body can be experienced as the fullest, richest, and most magical of places but also as the most painful and cumbersome, a storehouse of fears and inhibitions. To help the body become a magical cave, the two elements of breath and movement are necessary.

ES: Can you say more about breath and movement?

EP: Breath opens the body. Breathing gives the body an opportunity to experience and receive without contraction, fear, or frozenness— outside of the fight-flight-freeze response. To mobilise openness, I have to breathe. To experience the power of life, I have to move; open-ness necessitates movement. In sex, for example, this is the pelvic thrust, the rounded movement, which enables blood-flow and inten-sity. The wider the movement is, the more powerful the experience.

ES: I would like to add a third element, which connects to pausing: being seen. We all share a deep desire to be seen as unique. To create passion we need to make another person feel unique and singular. Once they are seen as unique, a passionate merging becomes possible.

EP: One of the central themes in my new TED talk[1] is exploring the romantic ideal that *I am chosen*. I am it. I am unique. I am indispens-able and irreplaceable. This is the grand ambition of love. You can experience this with friends, but in the romantic utopia, this is the big dream and sadly infidelity tells me I am not: I am not *that* unique, I am neither irreplaceable nor indispensable.

Eds: But in the restaurant, we are not your only customers, Eyal. You ask us to hold the fantasy, like Esther's magician, that we are unique. Because we can see you move from one customer to another, relating to each as unique. Very much like psychotherapists.

ES: True. Yet from the moment I create intimacy with one person, the air is full with the sense of desire and intimacy, with the possibility of merging. I will connect with you, look at you, and absorb your energy, robbing you of yourself. And I will materialise your energy into food: I give it back to you to consume, to reclaim the energy which was robbed from you, and you will also receive my own energy. I provide you with a capsule of our merged energies, and you take it in, allow it to spread in your bloodstream.

Eds: The model you offer is that of serial monogamy. Like in therapy, each customer needs to agree to suspend disbelief, not be consumed by jealousy yet still believe that you love them.

ES: To do so is to live the moment. The ultimate presence of here and now is the gift of the magician.

EP: The main difference between a restaurant and couple relationship is time. When in a restaurant I know that I am not the only one, but I really wish that for the five minutes you are with me I can hold the belief that there is nobody else. I know it to be untrue but I accept the story of being the only one, and enjoy the lie—which we have co-constructed. But this experience lasts moments. In romantic relationships it would have been good if we could say the same, it is never just me. But it hurts; we want this imagination to become true. The fact that you are choosing to be with me and to love me doesn't mean that others cannot enter too.

ES: True. When people get married, choice is often illusive—either chocolate or vanilla. There is preference: despite everything that I know, I choose you. Knowing everything that I do, I would be willing to allow for a centre space—for you and me. And you say that what creates the problem is totality?

EP: If it's *only* me, then when I understand that it is *also* me I will be shattered. We often refuse to understand romanticism as a function of our co-created imagination. For instance, in the past people married and had sex for the first time after their wedding. Today, people get married and they stop having sex with other people. It is a very different story. The choice of being the one and only is very different from recognising there were others and with me you will now stop.

Eds: Both of you speak of pauses and stopping, and in other places of death and impermanence as possibly a precondition for desire. Can you say more about it?

EP: I want to differentiate between death and deadness. First and foremost I work with deadness. In many of the erotic transgressions—be they infidelity or consensual—there is a force in the transgression that infuses deadness with energy, because you make it go in a different direction; make it into something it wasn't meant to be. It is an act of creativity and in that you defy death, or you defy stillness. And the vast majority of infidelities are an attempt to beat back deadness, which may be inside of you because you are numb, out of touch, or dissociated. The deadness may be in your relationship that has become alienated. Or it can be there because an external loss or death has suddenly become a part of your reality.

We say: "is that it?" Nobody can live with the idea that nothing more is going to come. We are afraid of the unknown yet if there is no unknown it means that you are already dead while you are living. And all over the world people who are in love or who are having an affair—they tell you everywhere: "I feel alive". That's connected to desire, the desire Eyal is talking about, of feeling special, seen, important, recognised. It makes us feel that we matter.

We are creatures of meaning and by being seen we feel that we exist in the eyes of another. It connects with a fundamental ontological question of "Am I desirable? Am I desired?" This is the one-on-one experience Eyal is talking about, in which I want to feel that you don't constantly think when you are with me: "Could I do better? Is the other restaurant better? Should we have booked there?"

ES: I grow vegetables on my roof, and there is this moment when the courgettes flowers finally blossom. They have this huge beautiful orange blossom. And as soon as this flower blossoms, it threatens us with its coming death. The flower is so gentle and tremoring that death lurks within its glory. In that moment I want nothing but to make love with this flower. We want to freeze the immense moment of the transient. Human beings find the transient desirable. There is a paradox inherent in romantic relationship where we wish it to be stable, yet desire a transient element, which threatens to disappear while it is still in its climax.

EP: This is exactly what my first book is about. [Perel, 2007]

ES: We speak of sexuality as if it is a profession, but sexuality is a symptom of a sensual way of being. When you live sensually then sexuality is part of it, otherwise sexuality is foreign. For me, everything is so sensual that I want to have sex with everything, to consume, and swallow, and ingest the world.

Eds: Why is it important to live sensually?

ES: It's not important. It's a horrible way of being which makes life complicated to no end. Sensuality disturbs you in discovering how to survive in this world. When you are sensual you are exposed, defence-less; you need to be in environments where you are loved and respected. Being sensual is not the best way of living. But it's also wonderful; you need for every matter to become spirit and for every spirit to transform into matter. It's not an economical method, but if you are a good storyteller you can prosper here. However, if you cannot tell stories about it you are destined to misery.

EP: I like Eyal's answer, I would however be more careful with the polarity of those who are and those who are not sensual. It's a conve-nient distinction, but I would rather organise desire and sensuality in terms of tension—towards sensuality, and towards the opposite—the pragmatic.

One is the process, the experience, and the other the outcome. You can have sex and feel nothing. Women all over the world for centuries are having sex and feeling nothing. So here is an experience that for some can feel the most delicious, magnificent and meaningful and for others the same experience can be felt as completely traumatic and violating, or no different to doing the dishes. You can take every juice out of sex.

I do think that we are born with certain temperaments, and maybe at the beginning most children like to be touched and want a response, and if you don't get a response your body learns not to trust. Consequently it becomes difficult to give yourself and you close down. Some people can experience the blossom of the courgette Eyal speaks about, yet they cannot be sexual or sensual with their body. Eroticism can be experienced in nature or art and in many other ways.

Sensuality is a language, but one that people can learn. I have seen people learning to open up in magnificent ways. Is it the same? It doesn't matter. They have never before known this realm of experi-ence and now they do. Experience matters because we are subjective creatures and experience is what tells the stories of our life. Without experience we have no story to tell, and without a story to tell we have no life to live.

Eds: Eyal, having experienced Esther, what food would you prepare for her?

ES: As soon as a person eats something his world changes. Food is not only of the body; food has a desire and a wanting. Food tells us the stories of where it came from. We all desire the body in order to receive the soul. We seek to eat the sea, and the sky, and the sun, and the earth. When we come to make love, we also want to take the spirit of the other and merge it with our own blood.

Esther knows how to feel. There is a feline-like quality to her. She is less interested in what she sees but more in what is churning underneath, in that which is becoming. Esther, you do not belong to places where soul resides in blood, you belong to vegetables. Why? Because the soul of vegetables is more elusive; you can feel their desire and yearning which they try to convey. Yet capturing the soul of a vegetable requires great wisdom. If I were to make you one thing today, I would take a turnip, steam it in water, and shape it into a square, slicing it into thin sashimi. Adding just four grains of salt and a few drops of olive oil, I think you'd be very happy.

Eds: Esther, would you like to add anything for dessert?

EP: As Eyal notes, food and sex are both cultural icons. In one of the videos I use for training, I show a woman who always felt unseen and non-existent. She never had an orgasm, because she had enough: his needs were met and then it was over. At the end of the session she shared how, when her partner finishes eating she places what was left in her plate in his. This was a metaphor of their entire relationship. I asked her to take an ice cream cone, and eat this ice cream all by herself while he watches. She was not allowed to give him any. This intervention was directed at helping her experience pleasure without guilt. When she gave him the leftovers, she didn't feel good about it; it was a strategy to prevent her from feeling bad, selfish, and guilty. It had nothing to do with the pleasure of giving, hence he never felt that she gave from a place of openness and did not particularly enjoy receiving either sex or food. Recently I received a letter from this woman, saying I want you to know that I never ate dinner with him the same ever again.

Sexuality is a window into the most archaic rooted elements of a society, and the most radical changes manifest around its attitudes to sexuality.

Eds: Thank you both for an alive, exciting, and inspiring dialogue.

Note

1. www.ted.com/talks/esther_perel_rethinking_infidelity_a_talk_for_anyone_who_has_ever_loved?language=en

PART IV

THE BODY OF PAIN

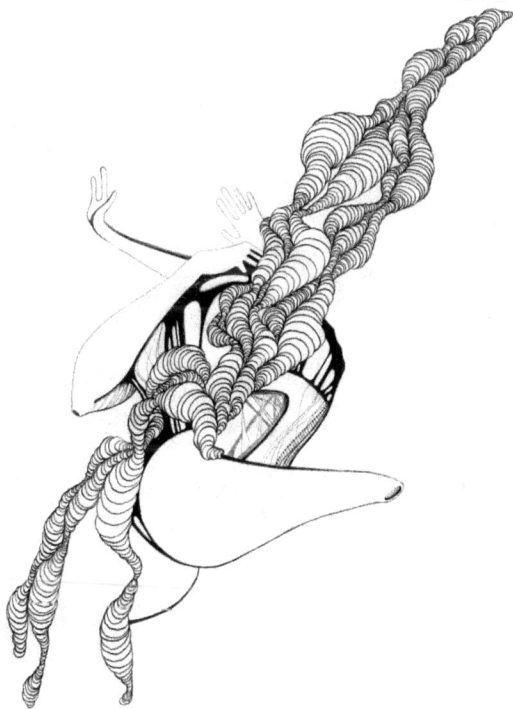

Introduction to Part IV

"Pain is a language of sorts, with its uniquely encoded messages.
It is a language written in the person's flesh, psyche, and spirit."

Adi Kashi-Kark (2011, p. 65)

P sychoanalysis and psychotherapy were born from the ongoing attempt to address the basic human condition of pain and suffering. The inevitability of pain, which accompanies life, manifests at its fullest when the body is concerned. Our embodiment makes suffering and pain impossible to ignore. Yet pain is neither emotional nor physical, it is an organismic condition, one that overwhelms our being.

Pain also seems to allow for novelty, for connection, it is at times an enabling agent for deepening relationships with ourselves, with the other and possibly with our creative force, with the principles of vitality and pulsation.

To explore and discuss issues of pain, creativity, and connectedness we have invited two talented women. Psychotherapist Shinar Pinkas has for many years worked both psychodynamically and somatically with physical, psychosomatic, and emotional pain. She discusses a bodywork session and illustrates some of the potential for therapeutic work with body and with pain. Alongside her writes and speaks Flamenco and Ladino international singer Yasmin Levy, whose prolific creativity seems to emerge from the depth of pain and her enchanting voice echoes hopes, disappointments, possibilities, and heartaches.

Following their individual pieces, Shinar and Yasmin met to discuss the similarities and differences of their work and perspectives, in a piece that not only illuminates issues of pain and love, but also explores the uniqueness of psychotherapy as a creative art.

CHAPTER NINE

There is no process in death

Shinar Pinkas

D uring the first few years of my practice, a man called to set a meeting. I practised bodywork at the time, gently feeling my way into words. I mostly explored the possibility of verbalising what happened there, during the touch-treatment: through me, through my clients—and through our shared work together. This exploration is still a major motivation in my clinical practice.

Any practitioner who ever worked with touch would testify that the field is prone to stalking phone calls. A man called, and he was strange, incoherent, confused, yet insisted on setting a meeting. I clarified that what I offered was a body–mind treatment and not sex services. How extraordinary that merely fifteen years ago in Israel it was unclear that bodywork and body psychotherapy were not about providing sex services. The man's response was flat, laconic, and uncharacteristic for a sexual pervert, and I therefore decided to meet him. A very thin man arrived, his clothes hung on his body. He impatiently waited for me to end a session with another client while he filled in a medical questionnaire. In these years, I used to speak to new bodywork clients before commencing the treatment, to better understand the best way to work. Commonly, people complained of physical pains or wanted to relax, but during the sessions other things would emerge, depending on what happened together, in the room.

The man did not grant me a single glance, impatiently he urged me to begin. I asked him to take off his clothes apart from his underwear, and I left the room. Before leaving, I put some music on. The man asked me to turn the music off. He was assertive, too assertive, verging on aggressive. He looked like a person on the edge. His eyes were vacant; his back bent yet highly tense. His hands were tight in a fist and his nails frequently scratched his skin. He seemed to have hurt himself. His body was lifeless: thin, void, black circles under his eyes, unnatural skin hue. In some ways he looked like a tight spring— trying with all his might not to burst. "I want you to touch me," he said. There was no sexual context to his demand. Nor something that sounded like a fantasy or repetition of an abusive relationship. His tone was desperate; his voice low, hysterical, he took short fragmented breaks between each word. I felt that I needed to put him in a safe closed space, to protect him from himself; I really felt that he needed to be put back to his cage.

I began my work with what is now known in body psychotherapy as resonance (Boadella, 1982; Boadella & Specht Boadella, 2006; Heinrich-Clauer, 2011; Looker, 1998; Rolef Ben-Shahar, 2013)—I used my own body, my own capacity for self-regulation to attempt to regulate him. I took long, rhythmic breaths; I searched for my centre point—from which I could move upon his body, my working surface, without shifting position. I checked inside what I was feeling with him: a huge need to give him life. I focused on vital centres alongside my own body, I checked where I felt able to give and to what extent. I searched inside myself for raw energy, one that was not channelled to any particular system, called it forth into my hands and placed them on his body. I started to move. Movement, for me, is relational— an expression of what my body could give while listening to another body—it moves the energy between the two bodies; touch creates the connection.

I feel an uncontrollable shivering in my body. At first it almost feels like seizures. My hand shakes. I know this phenomenon when the electromagnetic field underneath me is hot or when I am placed over a particular point for an extended time, trying to work with it, disentangle it, but here I feel no warmth at all. Cold emanates from the body; cold energy of a lifeless corpse. I feel that I am trying with all my might to blow something into this life of his, seizing and shivering as it manifests through me. When I feel that my own body reflects something that is not me, I can go with it. I can take my hands off another body and check if it suits me. I can also be there with a meta-control of sorts. Here it is too dangerous for me. Dread spreads over me. His body oozes cold and I start sweating. The seizures become rapid movements, quicker and quicker, and after a few moments of strenuous work I feel I am falling off my feet, I cannot do it anymore. I have to let go of him. And I cannot take my hands off him. I feel that I become a charger for someone whose batteries are completely worn out, empty and damaged, empty and corrosive. Something in his energy is taking over me and I fight, I fight for his vitality, I fight for my own life. Inside him I see a dead space, a place that even the movement fails to enliven. And I breathe into him trying to physically, energetically move this place, I try crying into it, feeling it. Nothing happens. At the same time I am trying to enliven a dead place inside of me, a cold, alienated and inaccessible place, giving that place life with another part of my body.

So engrossed I am with this inner journey of mine that I do not hear him. The man moans and groans with his low voice, heaving and breathing and weeping. Something shakes his body, something passes through him, as if someone is moving through him unable to leave. I am looking at him, part nightmare, part reality, while he mumbles, "death cannot be negotiated, death cannot be negotiated". This sentence will continue throughout our session and I do not know whether to respond and were I to respond, should I speak? Should I touch? Should we breathe into these words? Should I facilitate a guided imagery? I want to be with him without running away, although the seduction to do so is great, I am in a nightmare, he brought me into his nightmare and I do not know what to do to help.

"Touch me," he reiterates, almost begging, he does not speak to me as a person but as an entity. I hesitate to touch, fearful of connecting again. His body is depleted, lifeless, like a rag doll. And suddenly he moans; a heart-breaking moan. It is inhuman, and automatically I place my hands on him; putting a little bit of humanity on to him. "I am running, running, running," he says, "since he died twenty days ago I cannot stop running. He practised towards his military service, for a year he ran on the beach every day with his friends and he asked me to run with him but I haven't had time." And his body is shaking, struggling to extract fragments of words or phrases, when I am trying to understand and intervene he shouts at me:

> . . . no talking, no talking, just touch. I know you understand; some-
> thing in you understands me; that's what I want. But how can you
> know it, you are ever so young and still you understand, have you
> been through anything like this?

I do not know if he is asking me or just himself, and I focus on the
dead place inside of me and work alongside my fear that this place
will grow, and I am fighting it with my other parts, the vital ones.

It is only now that this session can be spoken of. I guess I needed
to be emotionally mature to write it; as well as having a firm psycho-
dynamic ground to understand it. How was I able to remain there,
with him, I wonder, how did I not dissociate?

I could only be with him because I was able to identify with him.
My dead parts identified with him and I could then become him
through these parts. What happened to me was that my own body
took a shape, a form, a movement, that were not mine. He had got into
me; I could express him through my own body and thus understand
him.

He starts shouting:

> I cannot stop, since he died I am running and running and I cannot
> stop, I cannot eat; how can I eat without him here? How can I speak?
> How can I smile, how can I work, how can I sit? Death cannot be nego-
> tiated; death cannot be negotiated.

A howling of a wounded beast. I want to seal my ears. His muscle
tone is so tense, it is impossible to enter, as if the skin is glued to the
bones with no softness at all.

> When I run I feel him inside my body, I feel I become him, I nearly
> don't eat at all, like him, every day I ran ten kilometres. On the one
> hand I am dying and on the other my body feels like the body of an
> eighteen year old. I am getting stronger, I am muscular, I do push-ups
> and sit-ups, I run with his friends and bypass them; I am in his place
> since he is dead.

And for the first time his entire body cries with him, and something
moves through him again, like a ball, as if something of his son's
essence, so I feel, is trapped inside him, unwilling to leave.

> How does it happen, how does it happen, what shall I do now, will I
> live his life? Only when I run I am at peace, only when I run I feel that

I am connecting with him . . . I don't want to stop running, I cannot
stop running even now . . . I am running and you are touching me and
it feels good, it is good, you are touching me or him, who are you
touching? What do you know? But how can you touch like this, what
did you go through to enable you to touch like this? Just don't speak,
just touch.

Something in me becomes clearer. I am no longer preoccupied
with questions such as who I am, who he is, what are we doing
together. Instead, I am searching for my ground; for my stable spot,
my cracked earth, my capacity to stand on the crack without falling,
without being pulled into it, to feel the instability and move with it.

Today I can think of Balint's (1968) basic fault, and I realise that it
was only from my own brokenness, my own basic fault, that I was
able to work with him. Balint speaks of a dark, deep fracture at the
bottom of people who are psychically damaged, whose wound is
deeper than any neurotic conflict that might be deciphered through
verbal therapy. This basic fault includes the psychosomatic structure
of the person, and people with such a wound cannot be worked
through with verbal interpretation alone. Something in my basic fault
could work with this man's trauma, in a manner that a spoken
dialogue would not have sufficed.

I connect to my ground and touch his lower abdomen. I can sense
my tectonic crack opening, wider and wider. Many years later I understand, or at least it feels right, that he asks me to plant him in the
ground, together with his dead son. He asks me to bury him. He asks
me to bury his own body and bring his son's body out of the cave, to
blow the father's spirit into his son's dead body. It is Satan's work that
he is asking of me, black magic; a desperate act of a man who lost his
son. I fight against this dark world, those shadows demanding this
deed; I shall not give up, for him; for me. I want to leave the room; I
have no concept of time, only that a long time has passed, long, long
time, not in the ordinary sense of time and space. I conjure up all the
beautiful views I have seen in my life; all the people who have ever
loved me; moments where I felt happy. For me; for him. Bats are
circling above me and their eyes are of an eighteen year old boy. I close
my eyes and manage to touch him in his grief. I am touching those
lost places that have died, places that may never live again. I blow life
onto places that might stand a chance of healing. I stroke organs that
would later become a lattice of scars. I cry quietly and bid him

farewell. He grabs my hand and I stand there, without moving. He lets go and turns his head away. I leave the room. A minute later he comes out and doesn't look at me.

I never saw him again, but something in me has forever changed. The grief of the world has got into me in its entirety, and something in the naivety of a woman who knew not death cracked open. Death looked straight at me, and it could not be negotiated.

CHAPTER TEN

A woman, singing to herself

Yasmin Levy

I am a happy person who sings pain. In hundreds of interviews not one failed to ask me about my sadness, "why do you always sing so sadly, why only melancholia?" For years I felt compelled to explain that I am not depressed and apologise for the fact that pain is the fountain out of which I draw my creativity.

When I attempted to touch happy songs, at my audience's request, not only did I ruin them but I also felt that was uprooting the joy out of singing, doing injustice to the song as well as to my soul, primarily because I was lying. People where happy but I lied, these songs were not me.

At some point I realised that there were two types of artists, some who were born to touch you through your joy and others who were born to touch you in your pain. From that moment on I was able to let go of my war against suffering. People are intrigued by the gap between my painful, melancholic, dramatic singing, and my spoken intermissions where I can be quite funny. I adopted this humour in order to help people "survive" my concerts.

I open my piece with this explanation because I do not wish to apologise for my writing, nor do I wish to explain, time and again, that I am also a happy person. I want to write about pain as it is alive for me, and within me.

Singing feels to me like being in a different world, I sing from very high places, fulfilling my destiny. It is me and my creator, me and my soul. I feel so strongly connected that I often cannot see the audience. If you could see a winged-soul leaving the body, it would probably look like that. My soul is hovering, but my body is ever so connected. My entire body sings, the blood burns inside of me. My body was born to assist my spirit in fulfilling its destiny.

A few years ago, I was in a Cesaria Evora concert, we performed together in the same festival. I saw a barefooted woman climbing the stage, speaking to nobody. Behind her was an arsenal of musicians yet she communicated with only one. She did not even greet the audience with "good evening", did not thank us, nothing. She just looked at the musician and sang, and the audience was captivated, ecstatic. I left in the middle of her concert, I was bored. Writing it now about such a gifted performer I feel ashamed. I wanted to tell her, "look at your audience for a moment, speak to them a little bit, you do not relate to us; we could have put a CD on instead of coming here". Today I realise that I could not yet understand, at that time I could not have imagined that twenty years later this is how I would wish to be. Cesaria had no words for her audience; she just gave us her songs, here and now, on the stage, giving birth to a song. She gave birth to songs and I failed to get it. It was her and her destiny. I still find it hard to believe that I left in the middle of the concert.

My father was a renowned Ladino singer. For me, Ladino remains my father's voice and his singing; it is my mother shouting Ladino at our neighbours or blessing us in Ladino. And the food . . . the food is Ladino. Since my infancy everybody connected to the same Ladino songs, singing it with repetitive gentleness. Their approach to Ladino was old, obsolete, archaic, and from there came the same style of singing and playing that wished to protect the Ladino as they knew it, like keeping a precious artefact in a museum. I have always viewed those songs as alive, breathing, kicking, full of fire that wished to come out. This vitality was the birthplace of my personal style, Yasmin, a style that I created for myself in order to bring the world Ladino songs in the way that I believed they should be presented. It took me time to understand why so many people in this community, who were so connected to my father, and supported me, were disappointed and turned their backs on me. I took something from them; something their mothers used to sing. As far as they were concerned, they have deposited pure and sacred memories in my hands; it was as if I betrayed their soul. They were so deeply insulted by me, when all I really did was be myself.

On the one hand, there is something important in keeping things as they were, exactly as they were. On the other hand it is as important to introduce novelty to an existing thing so it may sustain life in a dynamic world.

I come from pain; pain is the manifestation of my soul's purpose. Without pain I would not be a musician and if I were, I would not have sung the way I do today. It may be funny, but I believe that without pain I would have been pretty miserable. I hurt many things, some of which I understand and others I do not. Had I known I would have become a singer, my life would not have been half as painful. When my father died I was a baby and since then my mum has become everything for us, her children. As children we always received the best of the best, the newest, before everybody else did. Despite being buried under enormous financial difficulties in her life, nothing kept mom from boundless giving to us, emotionally and materially. The essence of her life was about providing for us and loving us. I remember how, at eight-years-old, I woke up in the middle of the night and on the way to the bathroom I passed through the kitchen. For the first time in my life I saw mum sitting and crying. I became a woman that night, and sadness entered my life. For many years I created an adaptation of my mother's life to me—because I desperately wanted to protect her. My mother always smiled at us but inside her she was so sad, she wanted to be a singer but could not.

Every musician I know today had known from a very young age that this was their calling but for me it all happened later in life; the understanding and the choosing this calling. I never meant to sing. I avoided and fought this destiny until, at the age of twenty-two, I realised I should rest from this war. I realised I was born to sing.

When my hurting and tormented Ladino was not accepted in the community I came from, I left the country, looking for different musical homes, and I discovered flamenco. There I found that my work was validated and acclaimed. I received complete permission to be the individual that I was. Flamenco told me, "we are crazy, be crazy too!" And I brought this craziness to Ladino. I am wild and fierce and my singing is wild; I live the song with everything that I am—my body and my soul, I can be me.

Searching, walking, stumbling and falling, and rising again, I discovered Tango too. My son was born then, and I would put him to bed at night and play Tango on my iPod, and together with a glass of wine I listened to Tango for hours. The night passed, four in the morning, five, and I felt that I found a lover, I had an affair and the tango was my lover.

In Tango, everything is full of drama, difficult and sad; I could not find one happy song. There is a very famous and really sad Tango song called *Los Mareados*. I have heard many takes of this beautiful song, each singer performing it with so much fire and drama, since it was an Argentinian Tango. One day, by accident, I listened to an interview with a very old singer who also sang this song. She spoke of a fascinating conversation she once had with Pollaco Goyeneche, a legendary Argentinian Tango singer. He explained that the dramatic and extravagant approach to this song was essentially incorrect. There was a man sitting in a bar with the woman he loved; and everything was so sad, because that day they would part. The man spoke to her quietly, uttering each word through his pain, with soft and small, but ever so powerful singing. This interview was a point of no return for me. I fell in love; I felt that in that moment I understood Tango, life, pain, and suffering. I found a home in Tango, I could be sad without having to apologise anymore. This is how Tango is, sad, and I am permitted to be me.

Today, with the life I had been through, and everything I experienced, I need not show my pain anymore to create an atmosphere, as I used to when I was younger. The need to impress no longer exists in me. I understand that pain is forever alive in me, that there is no need to look for it outside. It took me a long time to let go of this illness that saw me as home and would crash me together with it. It took over ten years and three albums for me to find my voice. I was thirty six and felt as if I was born for the second time; it was beyond all doubt that when my voice came outside from within me I felt safe. Before I became a mother I was able to afford it, letting my psyche reach those dark caverns where I was lost, carried by the wind like a leaf, without warning disconnecting from the world. Indeed I was alive and breathing, but also dead from inside; boulders filling my body and soul. I allowed my soul the liberty of falling apart, of withering and suffering. I knew that those dark places alone would allow me to create. I have reached places that without my beloved ones it would have been very hard to come back from. I was lost; today I no longer have the privilege of going to these places.

Music is the fountain and the core of what constitutes home for me. I shall stumble and fall many more times, but today I know not to take my suffering too seriously. With each song, no matter how many times I sang it, I commit suicide on stage; I live it from the first note to the last. I give all of myself, leave nothing for myself; yet come back full. The fear is that nothing would be left once the song is sung. Sometimes concerts are alive in me for a few days, but this is rare, it is a sense of transcendence that my entire being partakes in. When I was pregnant, for instance, I could not move my left leg before the concert and was in great physical pain. I limped, dragging my leg, and holding in the tears (to avoid smearing the makeup) and the time to go on stage arrived. As soon as I started singing the pain was gone. On stage I could be with the entire weight and power of suffering yet still feel light.

When I am with me, with my audience and with God, then pain does not deplete me and singing it fills me, helps me be alive and more present to my life. It frightens me when after a while it diffuses; perhaps this is why I need to continuously sing and I need the love that those people give me.

I learned to connect to pain through a very clean channel, suffering that no longer shutters me. Today, when I am a mother, motherhood precedes everything, but alongside this, the individual that I am—not the mother—has a purpose that demands to be met. And when I am joyous, I cannot meet my destiny. There is Yasmin who speaks during intermissions and another Yasmin who, as soon as she starts singing, fulfils her destiny. I can see how, in twenty years' time, I shall be at my prime, the most connected to myself. An overweight woman holding a glass of wine, with coarse voice, sitting and not singing to the people at all. Instead, she is singing to herself; a woman on stage with her deep air of connection to God.

CHAPTER ELEVEN

Dialogue: screaming into Hell

Shinar Pinkas, Yasmin Levy, Asaf Rolef Ben-Shahar, Liron Lipkies, and Noa Oster

Shinar Pinkas: Perhaps I can begin by sharing where my piece came from. During a course I attended, the trainer guided a meditation and I suddenly recalled this client, from twelve years ago, whom I completely forgotten about. It was as if he left the room and closed the door, and a door shut within me as well, and for twelve years I have not thought of him; and suddenly there he was, such a shaking experience. I remember how, while meditating, the earth seemed to have opened and I needed to feel that I would not be swept. I came back home, waited for my two young girls to fall asleep and sat for three hours to write this piece.

Yasmin Levy: How did he emerge for you?

SP: Well, I seem to have lost the memory of that meeting and all of a sudden it was alive and extraordinarily hurting. I went through a journey during these hours, which illustrated for me how when things have died for us and we wish to revive them, they need to come alive through pain.

Editors: Why pain?

SP: Because when we want to bring something dead to life it will only live through pain, we must go through it. It doesn't mean that there would be nothing else but pain, but the return to life, this necromancy of our deadness moves through pain, and was made possible thanks to the emptiness of the meditation.

YL: When I want to experience aliveness too it is through pain. Looking at my life, joy is often a hindrance, and meaning arrives when something is alive for me—if that meaning is absent then I am not alive. I see myself as a happy person who is full of sadness. Were the sadness not alive in me, I would not have been able to create. Pain allows me to fulfil my creativity. I need my creativity to live; I am my creativity, the voice that needs to emerge and the writing that comes. In the absence of creativity there is a void needing to be brought into life. This is life in its essence, without pain it is not a life. I am a mother and a partner but my body requires pain to exist, otherwise it is hollow. This is a paradox, but what nourishes me most, necessary for my existence, is sadness and pain, without it I am simply miserable and unable to create.

SP: Yes. Pain holds a deep emotional connection. Like you, I remember being in a Cesaria Evora concert ten years ago. I have a sense that women who really understand pain cannot be skinny, pain is deep in the belly and needs to be enveloped, like a baby, lest it becomes intolerable. And then, on stage, something about her presence, barefooted and wearing her loose dress, she opened her gypsy-like mouth, and shouted her pain, not disowning it, not simply saying it's here or not, but moreover declaring: I want to shout my pain, not moan or complain but just say it is complicated, as if she was saying: I wish to scream the pain of the world.

It is a lengthy process, but both in psychotherapy and bodywork I wish to engage with my conflicts, with my pain, with my imperfections, and it liberates me. Perhaps dealing with genuine pain also leads to freedom [Scarry, 1985]. Something in the barefoot unperfumed gypsy women, needing to survive, begging for money, refusing to be shamed, there is also aliveness; a vitality in a sense of expressing freedom. You dare to be free from the prison of pain, break free and express it, liberate yourself. It is like flamenco, where the upper body scarcely moves, only hands and legs while all else is held tightly; and it hurts, so yet again the dialogue between movement and pain, and for me when pain is expressed movement follows too.

YL: The essence of being, which is expressed in creativity, is bare of mannerism. This is also why Cesaria is barefoot; she cares not to please her audience. She is there, serving herself directly to her audience, this is me. You know, my mother joined me to sing this week. She is nearly seventy, her hair is white. She was never a singer, just a woman who left the kitchen to come on stage and sing. People thanked her so much for singing, as if she liberated something in them by not trying. Like my mother, Cesaria didn't sing to the audience, or to God—she sang to herself. I am not there yet; I am still bound by communication, bound by the desire to sell my music. I know that at an older age I would no longer care how I look or what the journalists would write. It would free me to serve myself without mediation or buffering.

SP: This is really interesting; all my life I wanted to be an old woman. I am always laughed at on birthdays because I take delight in growing older. There is something genuinely freer and full of grace at seventy when you just acknowledge what is, love it or not—this is me.

YL: And this is a death of kind. Letting go of trying so hard is an ultimate freedom, but also something dies there. What do we let go of and what we cling on to?

SP: To some extent, it is letting go of some attachment to life, but when you are willing to release that attachment to life you attract social criticism, since we also engage in a kind of preparation for death, which liberates us from this life, a binding too.

YL: That's why we call dead people deceased, there is a level of ceasing, severing the binds to this world, its mundane and foolish qualities included.

SP: Yes, this pain is released also when it manifests—and releasing ourselves from pain is also a kind of death; both joyous and sad. When pain surfaces and we embody it and speak it, we engage with it and at the same time release it and it releases us; there is genuine pain there, since pain is a deeply existential experience. We are born in pain; women labour in pain and the baby, who emerges into the world, experiences pain as the first encounter with the world. Pain is at the core of our being yet we fear touching it, we fear allowing it to emerge, to be shown [Meital & Stav, 2013]. Something in the total surrender to pain carries craziness with it too.

Eds: Can you say something about the relationship between pain and pleasure?

YL: I had a gush of creative energy yesterday and I composed a song, which doesn't happen frequently. I wrote something about a broken heart. The man left the woman and at a certain time she decided to assume responsibility, not allowing him to hurt her further. As I listened to that song, it was as if two stars collided—with great force. It began when I came home in the evening to my children, singing to myself, and this earworm bothered me and disturbed me. And as I waited for the children to fall asleep, warming my voice and sitting to play and sing, this painful song sung itself through me; I was hearing so much pain in my singing. But this specific story is not one that I experience in my own life; I cannot relate to it today with Yishai, my partner. So, as I listen and am blissfully happy, I also hear the pain— this tremendous pain . . .

SP: This is the human condition, raw pain in its primal state; this pain is rawness—not necessarily connected with a particular situation, it is rawness which expresses itself through your creative outlet.

YL: But I don't want to reduce myself to pain. True, the subjects I tackle as well as my singing are often about pain, but it is also about pleasure—these are the places where I manage to touch people. This particular song might be about heartache and it may scratch my soul, but pain is a vessel towards connection, a fountain also leading into pleasure and connection.

SP: My piece doesn't simply speak of pain either. While touching on death and loss, it also attempts to look at an existential condition. When you tell me about writing a song, which is not necessarily connected to your own experiences, it carries rawness with it, a pulsation; a nameless pulse. Suddenly I am able to connect with this pulsation and express something of it. We call it pain since it is full of emotion, but we may think of it as managing to tap into an existential issue. This is deeply rooted in who we are but not in words, and I was able to bring it forth and express this something. I manifested a part of me into the world. Some people will call it pain, others would relate to it as purification but these are merely interpretations.

I can sometimes sense it in my clinical work, my creative force— when I am able to join a pulsation in me or the other, something I know that had touched an unformulated experience for us both.[1] I envy you for your capacity to call that something a song, since it remains. While for me, it is tangible for a second, gone the next, leaving me yearning for that moment, which I share with someone, and neither of us is in each other's life.

Eds: Shinar, you speak of your willingness to open to those existential and painful places within you in order to meet another, can you elaborate on that?

SP: One of the deepest pains of our profession is that the therapeutic relationship is not fully realised; hopefully I am not the only one grieving over it. Many people who end up as therapists choose this profession since this is their essence. It is a very painful realisation, that the highest and most realised moments for me take place in the clinic. I wanted to ask you, Yasmin, if you are able to do so not only while performing or composing—can you reach those moments in other places? Because for me, it's not that these moments do not occur at all elsewhere, but not as intensively as they do in the clinic. It's painful, and perhaps it changes over time, but could these shared moments only occur within a certain setting? There is a sense of sacredness which I cannot fully experience outside of the protective sheath of the clinic.

YL: You know, two days ago I received an email from a young girl who told me that she planned on committing suicide but my songs made her change her mind. I was sitting, shocked, reading her email. All I did was write a song. I felt tearful, thinking how incredible it was. And then, after the overwhelming emotional response, it closed down. She won't be on my mind when I next write a song; I shall not write with her in mind or contemplate helping her. My creative moments are my own; at the depth of my creation there is only me, I am not fertilised by another. Here, you and I are not alike.

SP: So you give birth to your creation while I, within the therapeutic context, cannot be without the other. Writing is different than therapy for me. I have been writing my PhD dissertation for ten years, not a realistic time, and I am suffering there. I am supposed to give birth to myself, yet I need a kind eye looking at me there. Unlike you, when I don't have a kind eye being with me, writing becomes a process of dying—I write from a dying place.

YL: Why is that, Shinar?

SP: Probably as a result of my biography, I need to know that there is somebody there. We don't need to talk or touch—but being alone within these processes is impossible for me, I cannot do it. For a healing to take place I need another to be there. Just like when my daughters play, they don't necessarily need me to play with them, but they need me to be there, they need to know they have a benevolent presence there.

YL: I am much more guarded today. My partner Yishai and my children helped bringing me into normalcy. I wrote a song, yet came two-thirty and even though I was at the prime of my creativity, I then needed to get the children. Yishai balances my need to indulge the depths that I regularly visit, because he is just not that person . . . I have many more buffers than before. I genuinely appreciate my capacity to dive into those depths but am not flooded anymore; I carry on with my life.

SP: Do you have a need for your work to reach others?

YL: Well, while I am grateful that it's possible for me to live of making music, I am not attempting to touch anybody. When I wrote my song yesterday I wasn't preoccupied with thoughts of whom it might touch. Today I am not that influenced by whether people will be moved by my work, it is less dramatic that way.

SP: One of my supervisors once told me: "Shinar, you've left the clinic, you closed the door, and you go back to your life. What was there was there, see saw—up and down—now you have a life." But for me, every time I leave the clinic I experience a death, letting go of the union is painful.

YL: You take bigger risks here than I. There is a muse, and I write a song and turn it off, and it will continue to ripple.

SP: True, it is a riskier position because I enter and leave people's bodies and souls and am changed by them too. Sometimes I notice that I walk in a way I don't recognise or I am not familiar with this word that was just uttered by me. It is clear that I leave therapy with aspects that were not mine and with these I return to my husband and daughters, who need me to be a certain way. Of course I can also separate, but it is a subtle separation.

YL: At a younger age I sought these depths. Today, I am at a place where my psyche can reside without crashing. I want to dedicate a song to you, Shinar, this is the best I can do but also my simplest; I then wish to carry on with my own calling. It is a big step for me, to walk with these songs, accompany them, and then move on.

SP: Well, I am almost forty, and I am really ok with never being, to a certain degree, myself—ok that there are always others in me and I shall always be in others. It is who I am.

YL: I am astounded by our differentness and closeness. I too find myself inside others—when someone takes a song, allowing it to touch, he or she ingests me, living with me inside them; only I don't know about it. Moreover, this is neither my focus nor my aim. And the song I dedicate to you is Allegria, a very old recording of screaming one's spirit into hell.

SP: Screaming into hell is a name befitting our conversation. I am moved by your description of being inside others without knowing it. This morning, for instance, when I told my daughters about our meeting, they asked me who you were, and we listened to some of your songs, so you were with us. Not knowing it protected you. You don't leave your body; people take you with them but you remain unchanged.

YL: Exactly, I no longer want the suicidal connection. I used to surf it and be nourished by it; I don't want it any more. But also, when I am inside people—it is temporary. This young girl had a crisis, and my songs helped. Next she might meet someone new and blossom, and my songs may no longer befit her new state.

SP: I am uncertain about it; because I've been carrying you with me for many years. I know that people carry me with them for many years too. I am thinking about my own psychotherapy and to this day I have dialogues with my ex-therapist. I don't have dialogues with you, but when I am in a certain mood I may play a song of yours.

YL: You are there with my creation. But we have different motivations. You tried to help that man you wrote about, and I didn't. I simply expressed what I felt that day, and it may have resulted in helping . . . We are driven to self-realisation by different motivations.

SP: As an artist you move on without taking responsibility, like a painter who paints and then says: this is my painting, and whatever you wish to make of it—these are all your interpretations, your problem. But for me, my creativity emerged from and is imbued in relationships. It came from me and I too move on to the next thing, but because my creativity is within a relationship, it has no existence without the other. I am fed by relationships; I need them to be continuous, to have longevity.

Eds: It is interesting to note the difference in the directionality of pain.

YL: True. When I finish performing on stage I may have two more hours of this foggy, transitional state and then I go into my car and drive and it is over, I cannot preserve it. And as I am driving I may recall a moment of grace when the audience was with me, and sometimes I regret that these moments cannot be kept in a box to sniff once in a while. When my voice comes out perhaps this is what I need. Sometimes I do imagine that someone is listening to me singing and I feel understood, as if they join me in pain; and the knowledge of this recognition nourishes me. But these are rare occurrences. Mostly, my creative act suffices.

SP: Yes. You, Yasmin, create from within—you are inspired by a muse, by God—this is where your pain is expressed, and it touches others as a by-product; whereas I work within a relationship and the pain is only realised when it is no longer inside of me but within the connection; it is then that pain receives meaning.

Note

1. Worthwhile mentioning Daniel Stern's description of Now moments where " 'I know that you know that I know' or 'I feel that you feel that I feel' " (2004, p. 75).

PART V

THE BEAUTIFUL BODY

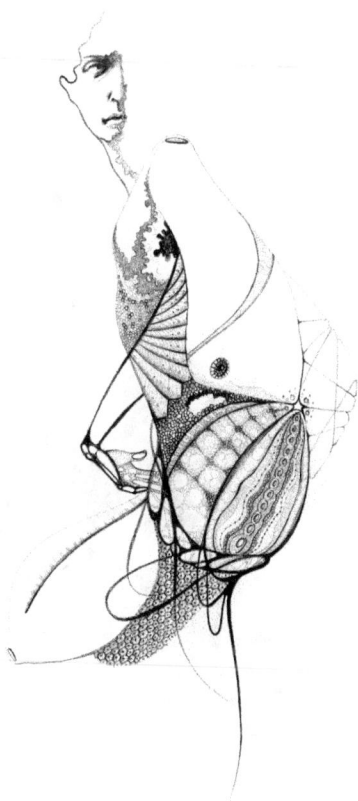

Introduction to Part V

I n his seminal work on aesthetics and relativism, *Ways of Worldmaking*, philosopher Nelson Goodman (1978) suggested: "If attempts to answer the question 'What is art?' characteristically end in frustration and confusion, perhaps—as so often in philosophy—the question is the wrong one" (p. 57). Instead, offered Goodman, the question should relate to the contextual, symbolic frame within which we consider art. The question should be "*When* is art?"

When coming to appreciate human beauty, we discover in its depths the dialectics between cultural values and the individual sense of self. The question *when is beauty* relates to the contextual lattice of values, beliefs, and interests that comprise our culture and our inevitable ties with it. In a society so deeply invested in consumerism, beauty tends to become a commodity, purchasable goods (Rolef Ben-Shahar, 2015). To discover beauty as a means of recognition and aesthetic appreciation of ourselves and the other, we may be called to first deconstruct cultural definitions of beauty (Orbach, 2009).

To tackle these complex issues, we invited relational psycho-therapist Esther Rapoport who specialises in working with gender, sexuality, and power dynamics as they manifest in the personal and socio-political arena. We were also fortunate to have fashion journalists and TV presenters Trinny Woodall and Susannah Bertelsen join us. Trinny and Susannah have done incredible work with women around the globe in finding ways of appreciating their bodies and discovering their beauty. The dialogue between the three is a fascinating document of shared attempts to cultivate kinder ways of relating to ourselves and others. The three discuss questions of truth, presence, mutuality, and the directionality of change with honesty and curiosity. Asaf joins the conversation between the three to support the dialogue as well as to represent men in this all-women conversation.

We will discover a chaotic world where the attempts to deconstruct norms lead to questions of identity and recognition, and illuminate the inevitability of context, out of which we can never fully emerge, but can still aspire to transcend.

CHAPTER TWELVE

Subjects of beauty

Esther Rapoport

F or many years, I walked around with short, stern dykey hair-
    cuts. This year, I have let my hair grow out a bit. I have also lost
    some weight over the recent months, due to the wartime stress
(I live in Israel) and the gluten-free diet I adopted for health reasons.
Ever since losing the weight and gaining the hair, I have begun to
receive numerous compliments from everyone around me. Everyone,
that is, besides my dyke friends, who find these changes in my
appearance unsettling.

Who does not enjoy compliments! I certainly do. But, I liked
myself just as much with the weight, and without the hair, as I do
now. As yet another heterosexual acquaintance marvels at my slimness and assures me I look amazing with this new hairstyle, what I am
hearing is, "Thank you for finally looking comprehensible, for no
longer confusing and challenging me."

Do most compliments women receive, whether from men or from
other women, bear the same message?

In the mainstream, heterosexist culture, women are complimented
for looking feminine: soft, slim, sexy, and elegant. What if I, a woman,
want to look androgynous, strong, and reserved, and to take up
space? What if I feel beautiful when I embody these qualities and want

others—not only butch-femme queer women but also heterosexual women and men—to recognise me as beautiful when I look quite out of line with the cultural norm? What if I want men as well as women to be attracted to my strength, my reserve, and my androgyny? To be attracted to me for, not despite, what I feel makes me beautiful?

Sometimes I fantasise about being a Big Black Woman or a Big Arab Woman. I envy Black and Arab women because in their cultures it is more normative to be big. I do not romanticise this freedom they have—I know it is not absolute: they, too, live in the global world where the ideal of feminine beauty is the white ideal of slimness, and feel ill at ease about failing to fulfil it. I envy them even as I am aware of their distress.

I would like to be a big woman in the world of other big women. I would like to look imposing and dominant; I would like my body to be giving off a message of power. I would not want to look fat in a world where fat evokes disgust. Rather, I would like to look big in a world where a woman's big body evokes admiration and awe, and turns men and women on.

Such fantasies are so rarely shared and discussed that at times I wonder if I am the only one who has them, and begin to question my sanity. Perhaps that is why I felt so elated when a friend from Gaza, who managed to get a permit to come to Tel Aviv for one night, nodded approvingly at a painting in my apartment showing a big woman with a chunky, unevenly shaped butt. The butt is directly in the centre of the painting, and definitely also in the centre of the viewer's attention because it is quite large, and of a peculiar, albeit realistic, shape. "I love this painting," she finally said, after studying it for a while, "I love how it shows the female body as irregular, it's so liberating."

My patient Mirit is upset because she has not been approved for the weight-loss stomach surgery. Her sister is getting the surgery, leaving Mirit the only fat one in the family. It has been bad enough to be one of the two fat sisters—the two of them have always been teased by the rest of the siblings in their large family—becoming the only one feels plain unbearable. What is she going to do? I feel distress as I listen to her. I cannot accept her siblings' persecution of her body or her complicity with that persecution. Why does she not rebel? Why can she not just tell them her weight is none of their business and they have no right to tease her? I feel angry at them, at her, and at the culture. I do not know what to do with my anger. "How do *you* feel in your body?" I enquire. She looks at me disdainfully. "What do you think?", she asks coldly. "How would *you* feel?" I know she thinks I am being mean on purpose: trying to make her suffer by forcing her deeper into an experience that I know is painful. On my side, what I want is to make room for her to encounter her body directly, away from the judgmental glances of her brothers and sisters.

I should have known better. To her, there is only one truth: she is fat, and being fat means being ugly and bad, hence she is ugly and bad. There is nothing to explore because exploring will not make her thinner.

Several sessions down the road, she announces that she has a plan: across the street from my office, there is a special gym where they wrap electrodes all around you to send impulses to your muscles while you are exercising; thanks to these electrodes, you can exercise for twenty minutes but your body reacts as if you did it for three hours. She is going to try it out right after our session. She is hopeful. I am thinking back to the time when she hired a personal trainer for a couple of months, then to the weight-watching group she used to attend, and those spurious weight-loss pills with all kinds of disturbing psychological side effects that she tried a year ago!

As she tries, briefly, one method of losing weight after another, she expects me to support and encourage her efforts. I feel resentful of this role that she assigns to me yet play it, reluctantly. I would like to play an altogether different role: of someone who helps make it possible for her to explore how she came to internalise the idea that fat means ugly and bad. How did the family culture develop where this was fully agreed upon? I would like her to disidentify, if only for a brief moment, from her family's fat-phobic assumptions that she seems to never once have questioned.

Alas, just as she is not allowed to feel, remember, or reflect when it comes to her weight—nothing but concrete action such as dieting, exercising, taking pills, or pursuing a stomach surgery—so, too, I am not allowed to ponder, ask questions, or interpret. Anything I say is experienced as uncaring at best, persecutory at worst. The only action I am allowed to engage in is the concrete action of supporting her in losing weight: saying, "Great job!" when she reports she is trying a new method, enquiring into the details of what exactly it implies and spurring her on when she begins to lose faith in it.

Should I claim my freedom by not complying with these expectations, she could easily come to feel neglected and abandoned. If I were to say, as I wish to so very badly, that we need to look at what weight means to her and how it came to mean that, she would accuse me of being distant and mechanical—doing textbook therapy—or of wanting to preserve the status quo where I am much slimmer than she is. If I do not care for her to be thin, I do not care for her, period.

The contemporary Western beauty ideal oppresses us whether we comply with it or not (Wolf, 1990). Insofar as we do, we are forced to invest an enormous amount of energy in attaining and maintaining the "beauty" demanded of us. Insofar as we do not, we have to face constant disapproval and keep fending off others' attempts to change us. Queer men have to meet the same demands as heterosexual women: be slim, hairless, and fit. Heterosexual men face disapproval if they are attracted to "lower caste" women—those who do not fit the beauty ideal. Sisgenders (biological females or males whose gender identity is in line with their anatomy) and transgenders, first-, second-, and third-world women, queers, and men face different forms of this oppression.

Yet we sometimes manage to feel free in the face of this tyranny. My body feels beautiful to me when I am experiencing an orgasm or profound relaxation, when I realise I do not feel tired after biking from North Tel Aviv to Jaffa, when I have managed to get a large sofa out of my apartment and down the stairs without anyone's help.

Adi wishes to show me a photo of herself in a new dress. She hands me her smartphone, I look at the picture and smile. The knee-length blue dress does suit her. There is an endearing awkwardness to her posture as she poses for the camera. Like a nineteenth century peasant girl who has never had her picture taken before, I think. I study her facial expression in the photo. It is one of sheer happiness. Can anyone be so absolutely, innocently, happy? I feel touched to the core by her joy. "Beautiful", I say, handing the phone back. She smiles back, mischievously.

When she first walked in, two years ago, as a twenty-four-year-old boy, her long body seemed lifeless and out-of-place. She had spent thousands of hours online, in virtual reality, always choosing female characters as she played computer games with people in other countries who knew nothing about her besides her being a girl. At twenty-four, life as she knew it did not feel possible anymore. When she became so depressed as to stop eating, she realised she had no choice but to pursue sex change, and sought therapy.

Adi is one of the few trans women I know who are able to like their bodies even before any surgeries. The first effects of the sex-change hormones were sufficient for her to start enjoying looking at herself in the mirror.

I ask myself if I am able to see Adi's unique beauty, or does she look beautiful to me because all trans women do? The freedom of choosing femininity rather than being forced into it, which Adi embodies, washes over me like ocean air, refreshing and invigorating. I adore her ability to only accept those aspects of being a woman that she likes: playfulness, yes, fear of sexual harassment, no; looking and acting sexy, yes, feeling she must care for others to justify her existence, no. It is impossible to objectify her because she is so fully invested as a subject in her desire to be seen as a beautiful woman.

Looking at her, I cannot help fantasising about being in her shoes. How empowering it might feel to be her! How I would love to choose to perform femininity as a liberating act! Take the seemingly simple act of removing bodily hair, for example. For me, this is an ongoing struggle. Sometimes I choose to rebel against the commandment to shave, which angers me because I fail to see the rationale behind it: the hair grows on the body naturally and is part of our natural protection against environmental threats—why get rid of it? At other times, I get tired of looking different from everybody else and getting the looks, and comply to make my life easier. In either case, I cannot win, because I am unable to ignore the commandment—whichever course of action I take, it is always in reference to it.

For Adi, the act of removing her hair has a completely different meaning: she takes it on willingly as part of the femininity that she yearns for. To her, shaving her legs is not an act of compliance—she is not yet, and not fully, a woman, by society's standards, so this is not required for her, nor is it an act of defiance, as it might be for a man— as she is not a man, and never was one. Hence, for her it is a choice, and an act of freedom (Symington, 1983).

I find myself wondering if femininity will forever remain, for her, as liberating as it is now. Will there be a point, after the surgery and the sex change in her state documents, when shaving her legs and putting on makeup will become part of the unexciting routine? Or will she continue to deeply appreciate being able to openly display her feminine identity for the rest of her life?

Relational psychotherapy is, for me, a practice of freedom (Aron & Starr, 2013). It is about finding, if only for a brief moment, an idiom that is uniquely-one's-own-in-the-other's-presence, experiencing the pleasure of sharing it with that other, and feeling the other's reverberation (Benjamin, 1990). In Margaret Atwood's *The Handmaid's Tale* (1985), a handmaid who has been deprived of all vestiges of her own identity and autonomy finds pleasure in sex with a lover, which is forbidden to her as she belongs to her master, even as she expects to be discovered and killed at any moment. The relational technique at its best can enable us, therapists and patients, to secretly enjoy moments of seeing each other's beauty even as the Moloch of the totalitarian beauty ideal is standing outside the door, waiting to extract his due.

CHAPTER THIRTEEN

The journey back to self-worth

Trinny Woodall and Susannah Bertelsen

C an I see my own beauty? Can my eyes see my face, my hair, my body with kindness? Am I allowed to show my beauty?

Together we walk with the women who come to work with us. We walk hand in hand with each woman. We strip together with them and reveal the stories of their lives and our own. We have been working with women for so many years now, offering them kindness, caring, lack of judgement, and permission to be beautiful. We allow them to look at themselves with kinder eyes by letting the stories of their lives and ours unfold. We found ourselves not once carrying their pain; we too were called to be willing to surrender to this pain, while still retaining our integrity and objectivity, in order to maintain our sense of self. These women and their stories go through us, and that is where the journey to self-worth begins. It begins when these women understand there is a process they need to go through.

When is beautiful?

We interpret all the messages we get. It is through these messages that we define our idea of beauty. This interpretation is individual; there is not a unified state of what is beautiful, because two different people, different societies will have a different look at it. When we work with somebody we ask: "What do *you* think is beautiful?" We try to ascertain what they see and value as beautiful. Cultural definitions of beauty can sometimes create obstacles for appreciating our beauty and goodness.

It may sound like a cliché, but we fundamentally believe that beauty is completely and utterly internal. The definition of beauty is so much more than a physical manifestation. We worked with many people who felt very unattractive because they defined themselves by the classical definition of beauty, according to where they lived; they allowed their culture to define them. At times, it has turned into a dimorphism of some kind, because these women failed to see anything good about themselves. In our work, there were times when we got somebody to strip down and look at their body. We asked that of them even though we knew they really hated every part of their body. It was a painful experience, but it was honest: this was their genuine starting point. At that point we might ask them to tell us what they liked and disliked, and with some women there was nothing they liked about their body at all.

People tend to judge themselves so harshly, that although beauty should be internal, we will start with the physicality, otherwise they will not trust our work. We will try to give them permission to find beauty for themselves by "lending" them our kind eyes to appreciate how beautiful they are. We might say, for example, "You have the most beautiful eyes, such expressive eyes." This process is a mental one, not a physical process, but it creates a bridge by blurring the definition between what is physical and what is psychological or spiritual. We are not looking for what is not good; most people are experts at this. We are looking for the beautiful, and we know we have got to find it—in ourselves and in the women we work with—so they can find it too. There, we try to open the door for their journey to self-worth. That journey allows those women to say at the end of the process, "My God, I am beautiful," something they have not even considered, and suddenly they can see that image. True, they have got all that makeup on, but that makeup and hair changes allow them a glimpse, a moment of seeing themselves through a different set of eyes. Here lies the magic, where a woman finds that moment on stage where she can own her beauty loud and clear.

Breaking points and breaking through

We discovered that the women who benefit the most from working with us are those who resist to begin with. Experiencing the shift in their own resistance creates a moment of reawakening, making them realise the issues they were carrying all along. The path is always an unexpected one, and unexpectedness is crucial and beneficial for going through a process of change. When we know what to expect, our minds will set in a certain pattern, oftentimes the one we are already used to; change cannot happen there. Resistance to change is understandable and welcome, and it provides energy to work with, as this is an emotional process. It comes to a moment of reawakening— a breaking point that brings about a breaking through.

We recall working with a woman who thought she was fat and big. We both stripped off in front of a mirror and we got a piece of chord. "Who do you think has a bigger thigh?" I (Trinny) asked? She replied: "my thigh is twice the size of yours." I went around with the chord and measured my thighs, and then hers, showing her the difference. My thighs were bigger than hers. She was shocked. We learned that with many anorectic women (but not only anorectic), until they could physically see something, they would not believe it. Doing it once is, of course, insufficient; you have to reinforce it, time and again, and with every part of the body. I went on with her and every time she said "my waist is bigger," "my arm is bigger," or "my neck is bigger." By the end she sat there bewildered, facing her cognitive dissonance, knowing her head was seeing the gap between her thinking and what she saw. She knew that I was bigger than her, but she looked at me as a tall thin woman. This was recalibration, a breaking point. And this is where we began.

First we realise how we see ourselves through distorted lens, how we are blind to ourselves. But this is not enough. Walking almost blind takes trust, and with that trust comes the ability to inhale the beauty we have inside and learn to believe it.

True, we spend a very short time with the people we work with. We want to support breakthroughs, to offer them a step on the ladder, hoping they would take it—wishing they would continue to cultivate it. We want someone who has reached that point of self-hate to see that she has a beautiful body, to walk through the studio in her bra and knickers, and be ok. And we will do it ourselves; we will do it with her.

Changing from inside out, changing from outside in

In psychotherapy, behavioural and external changes follow an internal change. We believe that change does not always happen from inside out. We hold the belief that deep emotional change can sometimes result from changes to the outside. Sometimes, we can facilitate external changes that would allow a woman to see herself in a kinder way, perhaps as other people see her. How incredibly painful is our ability to look at ourselves with the most unkind eyes! After all, we internalise the most harmful of voices, and often look at ourselves through the most vicious eyes possible.

We both have those days when we get dressed in the morning and look at the mirror, thinking, "Well, I don't look great." If we never had those moments we would not know how to relate to the women we are working with. This is a starting point. We seek to train people to look at themselves from a witnessing position, to be objective, and sometimes external change can allow for that distance, and this can facilitate a more benevolent way of looking at themselves. An external change can foster a safe distance to begin asking questions like "Can I see my own beauty? Can my eyes see my face, my hair, my body, with kindness? Am I allowed to show my beauty?"

Certainly, one of the hardest things to learn is to dress for your body shape, but once you know it, it allows a sort of acceptance of your body. The process goes through criticising the behaviour—not the person. We will criticise the way you dress, but we would never criticise your identity or physicality—we will never say anything negative about a woman's physical appearance, because we know she has done that to herself many times over, and this approach has not proved itself useful at all, only reinforced her judgmental behaviour and suffering. The journey into self-worth might involve emphasising what a person's issues are, particularly if this woman is unaware of those issues. But it does not end there. It ends with kindness, and with love.

Kindness and love

I once worked with a woman who had been very badly abused, physically abused and beaten for ten years of her life. She had a lot of scars.

I knew she was ready to show her body, but she needed to do it slowly. She told me her story in very small details, quite clinically. I met her for the first time, saying very little. On the second time I asked her "can I see? Can I see it?" and she went into the room, and I said "Darling, just take off your things." And she did. I did not give her any superficial caring words, because it was much deeper than that. I was with her, the world around us disappeared; she was witnessed.

We offer the women we work with kindness, which is hard, or perhaps even impossible to offer it to oneself. It takes a partner who looks at us kindly, for a long period of time, or a good friend, to make us feel beautiful and worthy. There are some younger women who seek a gentler and more supportive mother-figure, which they may have lacked, a mother who can give them advice but do so lovingly. Others, mostly more mature women, come because they want to feel better about themselves. And these women know they can always trust our opinion, and it will be honest, objective, kind, and non-judgmental. They long for a compliment, for physical connection, for an acknowledgment of their womanliness, of their worth. And here they get two women who care about them, and are not judging them; women who do not know much about them but still care about them. They know it and we know it—that the love is there.

There is an exciting moment when a woman we worked with goes on stage. She has not seen herself yet and she does the catwalk with her friends and family, yet her eyes are fixated in our direction, she mostly looks at us, with a complete feeling of trust. At that moment, this woman is able to see herself through our eyes, and she feels safe. It is like being a child again and feeling safe.

When we feel safe and loved there is little room for feeling shame and more space for acceptances and healing. When I (Susannah) look at Trinny working, she is completely absorbed, focused such that the rest of the world disappears. It is as if there is no camera, and she is completely present in that very second, to the other person. For me (Susannah), every time I work with a woman I give a lot of myself, I give my heart and my soul. I will take a deep breath, ensure that my legs and arms are open, let go of the unnecessary thoughts, empty my mind and just be there. There are moments where being present is difficult. Here lie the challenges for us and at the same time—the magic of acceptances, of kind eyes, of revealing oneself. During these moments we need to breathe and remember those eyes, and while we remain open, to accept our shadows and simply come back to open the door for the journey to self-worth.

Each of us has a different way to get to the same place, of allowing these women to go through a deep process. We serve as a safety net—so that they can fall back, knowing we will catch them. They know we will be there without necessarily having to say it. They know we love them.

CHAPTER FOURTEEN

Dialogue: recognising beauty

Esther Rapoport, Trinny Woodall,
Susannah Bertelsen, and Asaf Rolef Ben-Shahar

The dialogue begins with Esther, Susannah and Asaf;[1] Trinny joins in later.

Asaf Rolef Ben-Shahar: Does beauty exist at all outside of socio-cultural definitions? Is it possible today to look in the mirror outside the reflections fed back to us by culture and media?

Susannah Bertelsen: Certainly it exists, although in our culture beauty is governed by media and its preconceptions, and how women are supposed to look. What do you think, Esther?

Esther Rapoport: Well, based on experience I think it is possible; we have moments when we feel beautiful and we have moments when we experience another as beautiful.[2] There are moments when this genuine sense of one's own beauty is present, and these moments are quite precious, and are always at risk of being stolen from us by the culture, by its ideas. Perhaps we need to steal them back, to reclaim our beauty from the culture that tries to take it away from us; because we need to safeguard these precious moments.

SB: I think that the majority of women never had such moments. For many women there is nothing to take back yet, as they have never, maybe as babies, felt beautiful. We will be complimented for the dresses we are wearing and maybe if something is wanted of us; but I don't think people look in another person for what is beautiful anymore. Trinny and I consider the knowledge that one is beautiful as a bridge into developing self-worth; it is not a goal in itself.

ER: Perhaps this genuine sense of beauty, of being seen as beautiful is something about being seen not only with kind eyes, but is also connected to being seen as who you experience yourself to be—to be seen accurately; to be recognised. Being recognised at some very primary level; it has to be subtle and very precise.[3]

SB: Exactly. When someone recognises something in you which you may perceive as a core aspect of yourself, it feels more genuine. It has to be backed up by something more than the superficiality of words.

ER: Would you agree that beauty is fundamentally about recognition? Perhaps this miracle happens when one person can genuinely see another, not simply see another as a tool to meet their needs or a screen for projection. Like a mother being able to see something of her baby's essence and not just that it is *her* baby, not just that the baby makes her into a mother, or that she wants to love that baby. Rather, to be able to see her—it is something about those eyes.

AR: Can we hear about beauty and men? There is scarcely any reference to men in your pieces.

SB: Trinny and I came across very insecure men who have felt unattractive, but I personally don't appreciate a beautiful man in the same way as I do a beautiful woman, or think about beauty so much when men are concerned.

AR: I think that the shame that we carry as men is much more hidden. There is something almost consensual about your right and the legitimacy to speak about being beautiful or not feeling beautiful, whereas we hide it all behind wanting to be fit. I don't think many men go to gym to get fit; mostly go to gym to look beautiful and match a fantasy. Perhaps you as women are disadvantaged in being continuously evaluated by your looks, but you also have the opportunity to be recognised while we as men, we might not be evaluated by our looks all the time, but it's much harder for us to get recognition for who we are— not just what we do.

ER: I completely agree with what you say about the more deeply hidden shame Asaf, I think this is also true for queer women and queers in general. The upside is that you are not evaluated every moment on every occasion based on how you look. The downside of it is that it's less externalised, there is more hiding. Some heterosexual men have so few spaces where they can articulate this feeling, or even be consciously aware of this experience of insecurity about their looks, how will they look compared to other men, how they worried about being perceived by their sexual partners. Women have to deal with that more, but women also have more space where they can speak about it.

AR: Many men go to the gym in order to fit in with the fantasy of what we should look like and it's so shameful. It's just completely unspoken [see Strother et al., 2012]. I think there is something very lucky about you women. Because we are all vulnerable, we are all deeply vulnerable. And vulnerability around physical appearance is so accessible to you women. Sure, this is painful in many ways; and true—it is indoctrinated by men, but there is something tangible to contain and project your vulnerability into. As men we often don't know where to put our vulnerability; we have no legitimate home for our vulnerability. We don't have an obvious channel to put our vulnerability because we haven't been socially and culturally indoctrinated. That societal perception of beauty is demeaning and controlling is known, but there is something liberating about it too; there is a path onto which I can project my vulnerability, that's really comfortable. As a man, I am completely lost. Where do I put my brokenness?

   If the preoccupation with beauty results with potential recognition, while risking judgement and indoctrination, how can we offer more recognition to both men and women?

ER: This is first of all about undoing cultural influences. It involves peeling off these layers of fallacy and false expectations, of trying to fit into ideals that have nothing to do with who we are, of thinking that you should be beautiful for someone else. There is so much to undo that maybe by the time you undo some part of that, you are much more ready to see what's actually there, to recognise and be recognised. By adopting a state of a *beginners mind*,[4] where you really don't know what is beautiful, what is supposed to be beautiful, then you begin to see a person, whether yourself or another, man or woman. But if you are so locked up with expectations, standards, or fashion, you cannot begin to see.

SB: I totally agree with Esther, we both come from different sides but our approach is similar. Trinny and I do it very quickly and it's about getting a man or a woman literally undressed. Peeling off the layers, physical layers, and reaching a sense of vulnerability: "I am standing here naked, and I can't quite believe it," and then it is almost like being born again, being a naked baby, but with an adult perspective. It allows us to process the feelings of seeing ourselves, almost like reprogramming.

ER: I am actually struck by what you said, Susannah. You physically undress people and I am realising how this might be more similar to psychotherapy then I thought; the physical undressing and the psychological undressing. It does the job; the physical undressing is quicker.

SB: Physical undressing might be quicker but its results probably don't last as long, whereas in psychotherapy, because it's a slow process, the learnings are internalised more deeply.

ER: True, changes that are more gradual tend to be more profound and long-lasting.

[Trinny joins our conversation]

SB: When a woman has been on our show she can play back the recording and see herself, and the changes she had gone through. It can be an anchor, and she can retain that memory of herself, she can replay it at any time, and it helps cultivating the feelings she had then.

Trinny Woodall: There are different things that happen to women on our show. There are moments, before going on stage, moments of intimacy where she sees something in herself she didn't see before, and she may get a sense of her value. Susannah might have an emotional conversation with her, or we might stand next to a woman who realises the reality of her shape, and is shocked by that. And sometimes a moment will reverberate far longer with her than the catwalk, because it was intimate.

SB: The moments of breakthrough often have that element of recognition. And women, who from very early age felt that they weren't beautiful, tend to have powerful and profound changes.

TW: The majority of women arrive ready. They know us, they trust that Susannah and I are going to change them in some way, and they saw it, they know that a process will take place. They may not know when or how, but they are open to an extent. They know we will be honest with them. And because women generally have more things they are insecure about then they are secure about, it means a lot to them—what we tell them, honestly.

AR: Can you say something about the way your own bodies are used in your work?

ER: First, I want to say that I am fascinated by your work, Trinny and Susannah. I feel compelled to refer patients to you. Our work seems to complement each other nicely. As for the question; patients use of my body, they use my bodymind because I cannot really separate the two [Orbach, 2004]. I think it comes down to the quality of my being, of remaining in touch with my own subjective experience at all times, and what is invoked in me: the associations, the vibrations, and where these take place in me. I once thought that I could not help many women because I experience myself as a woman different from most women. I am queer; I could never fully understand the more feminine[5] women's experience. But the longer I have been doing it I realised that it doesn't matter. What is important is my connection to my own experience, and at times it even helps that my experience is more fringe, because it is as if I am a living proof that you can experience your body in different ways; or that you can experience beauty very differently, you can be attracted to different things. For example, I don't find very feminine women attractive.

TW: But what you are doing is judging feminine women negatively for their femininity.

ER: I am not sure that I judge them negatively. I personally find them less attractive. I myself don't see myself as very feminine and I am less attracted to feminine women. This makes for a particular kind of subjectivity that I carry, which is very much in tension with the cultural imposition of beauty, where femininity and feminine forms of being a woman are the desired ones and pretty means you have to wear a dress and high heels, wear make-up, and so forth. And since I neither see nor experience it this way, it allows me to bring something to the therapeutic space that introduces a possibility that wasn't there before. However, if I were more feminine and very much connected to that experience, that too would also be contributing to the encounter, albeit differently.

TW: Esther, you said that you never felt feminine as a woman. And I look at you and there is something very feminine in how you speak, and in your gestures. Perhaps you are missing something when you are holding this image of yourself, when in fact you are a feminine woman. I experience you as a feminine woman. And sometimes we get stuck with an image of ourselves which we formulated at a certain age and this is very hard to break.

ER: And do you think that I should break it?

TW: No, I am not indicating what you should or shouldn't do; I am just sharing what I see.

ER: You know, Trinny, that is fine. I think you are certainly free to see me, to perceive me the way that you perceive me and share your perceptions. But I don't necessarily feel recognised when you do. We were talking earlier about recognition [Benjamin, 1988], and I don't feel recognised when I am perceived this way—but it's a legitimate perception.

TW: Is it also your choice to hide?

ER: I don't think that I hide; I think that I am ready to be seen by others. But I wish to be seen precisely, in a way that respects and recognises how I see myself.

SB: We each need to be recognised differently. If I think at my own childhood, I was a pretty child and my sister was very clever. I was always the pretty one and my sister was the clever one. I felt so intellectually insecure because of that, that I compensated with developing a sense of humour, so I learned to be funny. We find ways, if you don't feel attractive or you don't feel wise, or you feel less than . . . in any aspect, you will find ways. Human nature finds ways to compensate.

AR: So how do we cultivate recognition?

ER: You know, we get distracted with daily life, we easily fall into our automatic patterns, and with all this cultural indoctrination it becomes harder. Because we want something from the other—we want love from our partners, we want money; we want many things. And we often become mindless because life nowadays is so complicated and we tend to act in ways that are not so awakened. For me the therapeutic hour is this amazing setting where I have committed to being conscious, to being mindful, to letting my best-self come out, and really invest in seeing. I want to see the other and let this miraculous divine come to the forefront. I am not distracted, and aside of money (which is a pretty major thing), I do not really need anything from my client. I can really be there [Stern, 2004].

SB: Yes! And it's that moment you are so totally in the present moment. You're in, locked with that person and focused. And the people that you are working with, Esther, and the women we work with—they know that. They know that in that very moment they are the most important person in our lives, and nothing else matters, and that is genuine. And they feel that, they can see that, they know that. It's the same as when we are working on television and there is a camera man who is focused on you. You know that at that moment you are the most important thing to that camera and the man or the woman behind it. It's so intense, it's almost like a love affair and unless these women really knew that what we do and say was genuine, there wouldn't have been a transformative experience. It is about being able to switch off everything else aside from the here-and-now.

ER: And to be in full presence with another being

SB: Yes.

AR: As we are coming to a close, is there anything you want to say before we conclude?

SB: I wanted to share how validated I feel in my work with Trinny when I hear you speak, Esther. It's really meaningful to know that, through instinct, we are being on the right path, because our paths have been very similar.

ER: Susannah and Trinny, I'm very deeply touched by what you said and I feel very much the same way, I feel that the three of us resonate with each other, and I too feel validated by this level of understanding and I am very much surprised. I did not expect that we would understand each other so well because we are coming from very different angles.

TW: Thank you all.

Notes

1. Asaf has joined the dialogue more actively to balance the female discussants on matters of beauty.

2. The single most influential psychoanalytic conceptualisation of the human capacity to apprehend beauty is Meltzer and Wiliams' (1988) work on aesthetic conflict, focusing on the importance of tolerating the enigmatic nature of the beautiful object, whose internality is not, and cannot be, fully known. While acknowledging the aesthetic conflict formulation, Anne Sweetnam (2007) discerningly points out that what is central to the aesthetic moment and its transformative power is opening up to the sensory experience as such: "Being changed by beauty requires sustaining the call, tolerating the surprise and yielding to its deeply sensory nature" (p. 1496).

3. Recognition is a concept Benjamin has written much about (e.g., Benjamin 1988, 1990). In her theory, to recognise another, one must surrender to thirdness—the mental space of intersubjective relatedness co-created by the dyad (Benjamin, 2007). In patriarchal culture, recognition is made difficult as men are taught to objectify women, whether partners or mothers, and patriarchal socialisation involves learning subject-object, rather than subject-subject, ways of relating (Benjamin, 1988).

4. Beginner's mind refers to a mental attitude valued by Zen Buddhists. To have a beginner's mind means to be free of preconceptions or set beliefs and to approach life with the innocence and infinite curiosity of a small child who doesn't know what to expect and is open to experience. (Suzuki, 2005).

5. I am referring here to some women's self-identification and subjective experience of themselves as feminine, without specifying how such an identification comes into place, whether it is primarily through psychological (e.g., Stoller, 1976, or social (e.g., Butler, 1990) processes, and with no intention of either deconstructing or privileging feminine women's identities or experiences.

PART VI

THE DIVINE BODY

Introduction to Part VI

René Descartes is considered the father of modern philosophy and the ending marker of the Renaissance. In his philosophical enquiry and through his radical doubting methodology, Descartes (1641) split the mechanistic world of matter—the *extended thing* (*res extensa*), which became the domain of science, from the spiritual world of the soul—the *thinking thing* (*res cogitans*), which was left for the church. In so doing, he freed scientists to engage with their enquiry uninterruptedly. Nevertheless, another unfortunate result of this radical differentiation was the split of soul from body, and of man from nature (Capra, 1982, 2002; Rolef Ben-Shahar, 2010; Withers, 2008).

While the early days of psychoanalysis involved some touch techniques, the vital body was gradually removed from the analytic practice, interventions became verbal, and the "talking cure" was fully established. Body, psyche, and soul—these have often become three separate domains of enquiry and interventions. Yet in many ancient systems of philosophy and healing arts, the relationship between the somatic and the spiritual seems not only possible, but crucial. Can we envisage a different relationship between body and spirit today?

We invited two men from very different backgrounds to engage with these questions and address them from their unique points of view. Renowned psychoanalyst Michael Eigen speaks of unity and fragmentation, and introduces his own search for the embodied divinity. He is joined by Rabbi Ohad Ezrahi, who brings a myriad of perspectives, from Kabbalah to Tantra to share his own view of the body–mind–spirit relationship. The theme of The Divine Body ends with a dialogue between them where they share some stories, agreements, and points of disagreement, where both biographical and philosophical experiences are weaved in the search for embodied spirituality.

CHAPTER FIFTEEN

Where is body?

Michael Eigen

W hat is body? For Saint Paul, in moments of Grace, categories dissolve. Words like body and mind do not hold.
The "where" of where one is is ineffable.

In *Lust* (Eigen, 2006), I write of moments when sensation is ineffable. In such moments, sensation is not simply a Platonic step up the
ladder to higher spirit, it is itself ineffable reality opening realities.

My little contribution to this discussion is meant to be suggestive,
without definitions. I have never been able to define anything. But, if
lucky, we can touch or tease some echoes of experience. I think of God
asking great biblical figures, "Where are you?" To which they reply, "I
am here." Where is this here? Do they speak from the fear or love of
their hearts? Do they mean the here of existence? Surely they are not
speaking of a Google map.

As soon as we begin to "name" body organs we are involved with
spiritual reality. Heart is perhaps foremost, good heart, bad heart.
Spiritual "systems" even locate good and evil in heart chambers.
Chassidic literature speaks of the good inclination on the right side of
the heart, the evil on the left. Hindu writings speak of a special heart
on the right side of the chest that is a place of spirit.

We could name many organs low–high, front–back, right–left, and their psycho-spiritual correlates in one or another system, for example, chakras, sephirot (Eigen, 2012, 2014a,b). Terms like body ego, body subject, body spirit, body soul, astral body, reverberate with multiple realities that colour life. The Bible says the soul is in the blood, which D. H. Lawrence echoes.

The more we feel our bodies, the more there is to feel. As a young man in a bio-energetic class, the leader tried an intervention in which I lay over his back, back on back, and he pulled me up, off the ground, and bent slightly forward, so that my back stretched and arched, a bow. I did not expect what happened. When he asked what I felt, I said, "Like a vagina." My whole body became a vagina. You might say, an imaginary vagina. But at that moment I was filled with ineffable sensation that brought me to another reality. I am tempted to use a Bion notation and say, I got a taste of O-itself, all through my body, which opened dimensions of experience I did not know before (Bion uses O as a notation for unknown ultimate reality, here emotional–sensory).

In roughly the same time period, in my mid-twenties, I was doubled over in pain on a bus. Where was the pain? Stomach? Heart? Gut? Not in any tangible location? It was the pain of my life. I went into it, felt it and felt it, doubled over, gripping myself. At some point, I blanked out, and in the darkness a field of light opened, wondrous Light, lifting existence, opening being.

Momentous moments, becoming a vaginal being, seeing the Light. Reference points that transform the feel of life.

When I was young, there was little difference between Eros and Spirit, except when acute guilt provoked tormenting difference. Now as an old man, there are moments when body turns into veils fluttering gently, tissues in velvet darkness through which ineffable dimensions with no names open, wave after wave.

It is not that body vanishes, more that it fades, softens, and more happens. Whatever the discontinuities, there is also fluidity between dimensions.

Here is one moment, in which a certain "flow" occurred between dimensions of experience. Kirk rubbed his shoulder and spoke of a pain he felt just under the joint ball, where it meets torso. After a time the pain spreads into chest and he speaks of heart pain, now rubbing his chest. I am aware he is under treatment for elusive physical difficulties and wait it out. He said something hard to hear about "ghosts", pains as ghosts, as they slid from shoulder through chest.

I had a series of nearly simultaneous thoughts, sensings, visions. Pains as ghosts of emotional trauma, mute impacts seeking–resisting acknowledgement. Ways the stress of feeling from infancy on pinch nerves, bones, muscles, organs. Bion (1994) says the core of a dream is an emotional experience. Our body is an emotional body and language is an emotional language. We lack capacity to work with feeling well and tend to suffer from partial emotional indigestion. We do not know what kind of pain is being dealt with how. I feel my breath has got somewhat shorter and faster as if feeling Kirk's pain a little.

When I came back into focus (the above thoughts a kind of daydream) I hear Kirk speaking of the pain of life. Agony felt all life long as part of existence. The shoulder pain he came in with dissolved into pain hard to localise and what he called his heart liquefied. He spoke of pain as a kind of pool in the centre of his chest that radiated outward through a psychic body. At this point, what some call physical, emotional, psycho–spiritual meld. Kirk broke into tears and in moments was sobbing from his heart. But what heart? The physical organ? Emotional organ? Spiritual pain?

Here is another example of fluid transformational processes working across dimensions with a man, Harry, who sought help after several hospitalisations. He eventually became hospital and medication free (Eigen, Chapter 3, 2007). The momentary level and tone was different from Kirk's, but one feels interplays between inner-outer realities that touch feeling and bring spirit to another place.

Harry felt his words killed people but he was stymied because he did not see anyone die when he spoke. He felt he had no impact. He would begin to die out and watch his emotional-self go under.

At the time I wish to share, we were sitting quietly, listening to our breathing. There is noise outside. My office is on the ground floor facing the street. A child cries and a mother chastens it, a delivery man chains his bicycle to the bars of my window. Harry breaks into tears, weeps and weeps, sobbing thoroughly for the first time and says:

> The mother yelling at the child was too much. When I heard the bike chains I thought, she is chaining the child. I have an urge to step outside and breathe, to unchain the child. I want to give that mother a

softer voice. When I hear her voice I stop breathing. My soul stops breathing. My breath contracts around the pain. I'm breathing cautiously, breathing around the pain. My breath cushions the pain . . . Now my chest is starting to relax. Soul is in my chest, returning through my chest.

I too cringed at the mother's metallic, scraping tone, my insides tightening, soul tightening, all through my body. A tongue lashing is a kind of beating. The emotional and physical meld. When Harry and I thawed out some, my hand involuntarily went to my heart. In one moment, spirit leaves, in another begins to return.

A few moments later, Harry fears that the child outside has stopped breathing. Does he mean a child within has lost spirit? We breathe around the pain, contract, find ways of surviving. For the moment, everything is in a breath. I think of the breath of life in the Bible, Ruach Elohim, God's breath-spirit enlivening life, enabling us to be.

There might be ways we stop breathing, never breathe again. Feeling has breath as well as taste buds. Our literal body might go on breathing in restricted ways, enough to get by, but emotional breath and taste may be damaged. Can you imagine a person who has stopped breathing emotionally? I have worked with people where this is so, and know places in myself where this is so. In Kabbalah, emotional life is associated with *ruach*, breath, emotional level of spirit (Eigen, 2012).

What is happening with Harry in the incident above? It is one moment in which he is coming alive in a new way, a moment in the birth of experience that spans dimensions, emotional soul awakening, heightening spirit. We are together resonating to sound, shrill yelling, metal chains. One moment binding, loss, another recovery. Sound runs through our bodies, giving birth to image, psychic sensing. Something is happening. The Bible links new birth with a child within. With Harry the child begins to thaw out and breathe with the going and coming of spirit, little bursts of time. We sit together, permeable, ready for more.

I would like to add a word about images of up and down, for example, dreams of being in the subway or flying in the air. One person felt his body a drill going into the ground, where he discovered a hidden subway system that no one knew but him. A magical world under the ground in which he could come and go as if invisibly. The same person also dreamt he could fly, so that his body was amphibian, now below the earth, now above it.

Flying and living underground express a need to escape the pain of living on earth. But they are more, suggesting also the life of spirit, including our double sense of being both above and below. Eyes as a centre of consciousness above, mouth and body with centres below (e.g., heart, gut, genital mind-spirit). We are made of multiple centres of experience. Ascent-descent is one of a number of organisers. We both subtend and transcend ourselves. Individuals report out of body experiences, on the one hand. While, on the other hand, attention can be placed on body surfaces and insides in ways that open infinities of feeling. The more one focuses on body areas, inside or out, the more nuances of being one discovers. Varying qualities of attention add to the taste and tone of experience.

Sensing has tended to be a second-class citizen in Western epistemology, low on the intellectual–spiritual scale. It is often taken for granted, that one transcends the senses to reach deeper dimensions of intuition and spiritual development. At the same time, sensation is a field of revelation, opening worlds that enrich one's sense of living. The term "sense" is one of those uniting words that run through multiple dimensions of experiencing: the five senses, a sixth sense, common sense, sense as meaning, and as Freud notes, consciousness as a sense organ for the perception of psychical qualities. Worlds that keep opening the more we open to them. One even may have a sense of God, a God sense with no end. We are all explorers of where head–heart–guts bring us, and much more (Eigen, 2014a,b).

The body visible is mostly invisible. Feeling touches us from unknown places or no place at all. It is not easy to pin ourselves down and undulating waves of body feeling are part of life's elusiveness, a sense including the rise and fall of spirit that is part of a rhythm of faith.

CHAPTER SIXTEEN

In my flesh I shall see God

Rabbi Ohad Ezrahi

My teacher, Rabbi Zalman Schachter Shalomi, who recently died, was an old man. In his last years he told us how every morning, he was full of awe and wonder from waking in up. Once he told us:

> Each morning when I wake up I open my eyes, realise I am awake, alive, that I have another day, and I say "Ribono shel olam, you decided to be rabbi Zelman for another day? I will give you a nice ride in Zelman!"

Severing the connection between body and spirit is a strange thing indeed. For any spiritual awareness we experience is mediated through the body—our brain with its electric and neural pathways is of the body, our feelings are of the body; even people who undergo out-of-body experiences are aware of it through their body. The body is a centre of consciousness, gathering all that we are able to be mindful of. The question is that of density, what is the density of what we are conscious of. We can be conscious of highly dense, material things, as well as for sparser aspects: aesthetics, rhythm, emotion. Subtler still are energetic sensations, ideas, dreams, and archetypes. There is a gradient of awareness from the dense to the subtle, and different people are willing and able to relate to different levels of reality. But still, reality itself is all of it together, from matter to void, and as long as one is alive it is through the body that we become aware of it all.

We can demonstrate it through the *frog parable*. Frogs are known to only see objects that are big enough to be a threat (a predator), or small enough to be their food. Naturally, the eyes of frogs can see the objects in-between but the brain does not respond to it, censoring irrelevant information. Our eyes too (as well as the rest of our senses) censor what we deem as irrelevant to form a cohesive picture of reality. I ask myself what level of reality do I open myself to experience? To which levels do I allow entry into my consciousness? What is regarded as spiritual is thus connected to the body for the simple reason that we are people inhabited in bodies, and all spiritual experiences are processed by our brains. Even when we lack conceptualisation, the experience is there—and it is expressed as a living body experience.

The phrase "From my flesh I shall see God" comes from the book of Job. The mystic Hassidic movement interpreted it as saying—inasmuch as I see my own flesh, from that I can see God. It is through our own flesh-eyes, through our bodily existence, that we can see God, that God was created in the image of man. Our flesh is the filter that enables us to relate to divinity.

In the Kabbalah we are taught to view our own body as a divine manifestation, of godlike presence, the thing in-itself realises itself and embodies itself in the world. This is a revolutionary perspective: the transformation that a person undergoes as he or she becomes more realised is not one of escaping from the body, rather it is a process in which I start to realise that reality itself, including myself, is in fact divine already. I see Plato's perspective on the body, as the psyche's prison, as faulty. The body is the realisation of the psyche, and of God. In our dreamlike platform that we call reality, as long as I am realised in this world, my realisation is nothing else than divinity, only a denser form of the divine.

I materialised, coming from subtler spheres I materialised into this reality through my embodiment. The soul materialises and realises itself as body, not unlike the rain realising through different forms. When we descend into becoming a body, the soul pours down like rain; we are not caged in our body—rather we become embodied.

The mind–body split is therefore a learned one. We are born with a wide range of sensations and feelings, learning with time to avoid many of these. Our body receives volumes of information, which we narrow down through materialistic social pressure, resulting in the narrowing of consciousness. Such narrowing does not bring us joy, we can survive it but we cannot thrive. Our consciousness manifests in our body and we are called to note that which we have learned to ignore, paying attention to subtler and subtler spheres of existence, allowing us a richer way of being.

For me, life asks us to fully live, relating also to the level of sacredness. Sacredness is not elsewhere—but right here, it is an in-depth plunge into the here-and-now of reality. This was the original Hassidic interpretation of Kabbalah: The Maggid of Mezritch, for example, in relating to Aziluth (the divine world of Emanation), said: "Aziluth is here". Aziluth is not somewhere in some heavens or sky above. It is right here—only sinking into the depth of what is already here. We are all walking in heaven already, walking amidst divinity; we are God walking within its own divinity and all that prevents us from sensing it is our lack of faith, we doubt ourselves, we belittle ourselves.

We are accustomed to approaching ourselves violently, to see change as resulting from violence. If my own body, Ohad Ezrahi, is too fat, I need to starve it, to force a policing diet upon it, instead of listening inwardly. Often we do not like something about our bodies—it is too fat or too thin, has cellulite, our breasts are too big or too small, penises too big or too small, it is endless, and we each becomes a harsh judge of our body. We are used to self-abuse and self-violence towards our body, to cut it through plastic surgeries instead of listening, rather than developing curiosity. Listening to the body is not a simple thing, it begins, I think, with developing curiosity, with not knowing: I know there is a wisdom here of which I am yet unaware, something attempting to be spoken. Is there a distress here? Is my body trying to say something? Is there a language I am not familiar with? If my body is too fat I may approach it curiously—how come I am realised in this world as I do? What is the secret of this manifestation?

When I look at God through this lens, divinity manifesting in this particular form, what does it mean? Why am I like this? Listening to our body like this I become curious, learning to accept how I am. I may even celebrate it—if I did not look the way I do, who would? It is my job to look like I do. Sometimes this curiosity may bring us insights about ourselves, for instance realising I am fat since I want to have "weight" in this world, to be of significance, to occupy space. In this way self-hate may gradually shift into curiosity for the realisation of divinity in my own unique shape and form.

This approach to divinity can also be examined through sexuality. Sacred sexuality is a meeting of flesh, skin to skin, liquids to liquids, and when we experience our body as a manifestation of divinity we also experience the other as such. It is the same divinity realising itself in different bodies and then the meeting between bodies becomes a sacred, divine merging. Can we perceive our genitals as sacred instruments, allowing us ecstatic pleasure, meetings that enable us to expand beyond the boundaries of self, to break through our narrow perception of ourselves? Sexuality is one of the entry gates into our innate bodily and divine experiences. The sexual drive is so powerful since it drives us to expand to the vastness of reality and to participate in the creation of life (including the making of a child). In Kabbalah, we see every sexual meeting as a unification that creates some form of life. In fact, the cosmic force of life pulsates through our sexuality, urging us to leave our encapsulated self and join a meeting with another. And there is more to sexuality; every encounter is in fact an intercourse, two selves expanding their narrowed existence and creating a self that is comprised of different bodies. We meet with our eyes, we meet when we talk, the world is full of magnificent intercourses.

When we can see divinity in the eyes of the other we unite with him. Otherness is frightening when I fail to see God in it, when I am unable to see the other as part of the divine unity. Naturally we look for ways to overcome otherness. War is a failed attempt to overcome otherness by the destruction of the other. When I can see the other as part of this wholeness, even if he is my enemy, I can realise our shared being. We move between love, fear, and love all the time and when we recognise otherness we contract and fear takes over. Does the other pose a threat for us? When we make love to the other, we make the other part of the wholeness and then we are together, we are no longer frightened, this is how love is created, and this is how we transcend beyond fear to a meeting with the other, into this oneness.

The Hassidic interpretation of Kabbalah relates to reality as an embodiment of the divine, and at the same time recognises that the divine is infinitely expanding, way beyond mere reality (Kalamish

Shapira, 1961). This complete acceptance of reality is a form of panentheistic approach. Although Kabbalah does not attempt to be a therapeutic method per se it still carries many therapeutic side effects. When we plug into such consciousness, many blockages, obstacles, and fears are removed. Ill health is created by blockages. Any illness is in fact seen as a type of energetic block, something that is no longer flowing. Looking at myself, I may recognise a certain problem and a desire to change it, to fix that problem. Both the problem and the desire to change it are divine manifestations. Wanting to change what is, is no better than what is—both are part of the reality that I accept in its totality. This is a type of recognition in various processes—this moment, in the here and now, including the difficulties and the vectors seeking to change it. That you are perfect just as you are does not mean stop changing, both your current state and your desire to change are perfect, are equally divine, equally sacred. Accepting reality is accepting its innate change, and this is the meaning of reality—of what is.

When we are able to accept all, we no longer fear who we are or what people will say about us, we no longer fear flowing, living, laughing, and crying, expressing our passion or our emotions, we are no longer afraid to be who we are. It is then that we truly meet our shadow, all those parts of us that we were unwilling to meet. The shadow ceases to be a monstrous threatening being and becomes a space of huge curiosity. What is being held in my shadow? If we know how to work with our shadows, with our darker, oppressed, and repressed aspects, peeling their skin and touching their essence, recognising which are the parts we need to reclaim in order to live life more wholly, fully, and undivided, then we do not need any splits anymore; then God manifests as all that there is. With simplicity.

CHAPTER SEVENTEEN

Dialogue: down the mountain

Michael Eigen, Ohad Ezrahi, Asaf Rolef Ben-Shahar,
Liron Lipkies, and Noa Oster

E ditors: What in your personal life made you interested in the
connection between the spiritual and the embodied? Or the
somatic and the spiritual aspects of it?

Michael Eigen: It was nothing planned, it was just spontaneous, but I
think there was never a disconnection. When I was reading philosophy I was surprised that so many philosophers seemed to make sensations second rate citizens, lower than thought. It was as if thought was
the crown and sensation at the bottom. But sensation made me feel
alive, sensation brought colour into life, sensation was bubbling over
with life; sometimes scary, at other times ecstatic, and sometimes pleasurable or painful. Sensation seems to be basic to feeling alive. In my
late teens, when I started having sex I felt God in sex—I didn't feel a
conflict. Later on it occurred to me that there might be a conflict
between sex and spirit. But in the actual feeling of sex I would see
God, a divine experience. I eventually learned about the Kabbalah's
link between divinity and Eros. The Greeks saw the connection but
somehow sensations were downplayed as second class citizens. Even
Chabad portrays the animal as lower and intellect and spirit higher.
Yet the animal saved my life. Feelings I got from my "animal body"
have been divine, ineffable. They gave me much fullness in life, a

sense of beauty and creative power. I don't think I could have survived without the wonder such feelings evoked. I feel I could have survived without thinking, but not without sensing.

Ohad Ezrahi: Thank you Mike—it was very fascinating, because for me it was quite the opposite. I grew up in nature and close to the natural world, but when I began my spiritual searching at fifteen I was already in some kind of a struggle between my spiritual parts and my bodily parts. I remember myself upset with my physical body, with needing to eat and do all these physical things. I felt like in jail, a slave to needs that no one asked me if I actually wanted, forced to take care of this kind of body. I wanted the freedom of spirit, liberated from the needs of the physical body. So my spiritual path started with a deep search for freedom, and part of it was freedom from the physical world. I later discovered Kabbalistic worldview with its cosmic Eros, but even then I tended to see the split, arriving at a junction of needing to choose between loving my body or loving God. There is always a risk to choosing a spiritual path on account of the physical one, and that regarded to food, sex, money, to anything that was of the earth; the needs of being in the world as a physical being. It took me many years to climb that mountain, and I don't know if I have reached the peak, but I climbed quite high. Standing there, I looked around and then realised, "oh, God is actually in the valley". I then started a long journey of descending down the mountain, agreeing to be in this world, agreeing to be in my body, to deal with money, to have an apartment, to be a sexual being, to fully claim it, to feel that this is divine.

During a journey to the desert, three years ago, one morning I looked over the desert and from far away there was one stone that was calling me, it was a stone like any other but I felt that I needed to go and see that stone. It was flat stone with two small grooves in it, looking like a seat. So I sat on it, and it was perfectly curved like my bottom, as if someone made a print of my bottom. What was the stone saying? As I was sitting, it occurred to me: I have a place in this world. This is the divine relation for me, in the stone, in the material world I am invited to be.

ME: It's interesting, because I find the mind more of a prison than the body. Certainly, the body is a prison because we're going to die. I am an old man. I'll be seventy-nine in a few days, and I experience all kinds of conditions that elderly people have, so I understand that each moment is a gift. And although death is near, and I am aware that when the body goes I go, for me the mind is still the bigger prison. An important question: how does your mind use you and how do you use your mind? The affective attitude with which you approach your mind, body or anything is central. If your attitude is filled with self-hate, if you cannot love yourself, if you harbour hate or too much envy and jealousy of others: your mind is a prison. If we approach ourselves with poor affective attitudes, such attitudes inform our whole body. A hating attitude can twist one's body out of shape and twist our relationships out of shape. How one approaches oneself is a significant challenge.

OE: I agree, the mind is certainly a bigger prison. At the same time, I feel that when we speak about the body we need to be sober about it, because the mind and the brain are of the body too.

ME: I am not talking about the head, but about experience and consciousness: how it feels; not where it is located but how it feels.

OE: For me, the journey of learning how to appreciate this divine incarnation was a sobering realisation that every spiritual experience that I had was actually happening in my body. If I am looking at the wholeness of what it is to be human I have to include all the reams, from the most subtle to the most carnal and say this is all part of me, and part of experiences I had while living as a body.

ME: Let me illustrate what I mean when talking about experience and consciousness. A patient with a transcendence psychosis lost his body and talked about being taken over by other minds which were not inhibited by time or space. Other minds ran through the universe invisibly with no barriers. This contrasts with an opposite kind of psychosis in which one is totally mired in one's body and lost in body functions. The notion of ascent-descent can be helpful in picturing consciousness going in and out of parts of body. In psychosis these movements can be very scary. There are many ways mind and body can relate and un-relate to each other. Aspects of consciousness can be amorphous with body, or unable to escape body, or not be able to get into it. Freud, in his genius, tried to fantasise developmental stages—oral, anal, phallic, genital—as ways mind, spirit, consciousness, psyche gets into body, incarnates, concentrates in different zones. Zones of incarnation.

Eds: So, for you, Mike, consciousness has a very dynamic quality.

ME: There are different aspects to consciousness. Now it's free-floating, here, there, now it's in body and now out of body, now in this organ, now in that organ. Consciousness can be in my skin, eyes, mouth . . .

I liked your reference to the biblical character Job as a mystic, Ohad. I too see Job as an adventurous mystic and my interpretation is that his losing everything should not be taken literally. It is like he is losing all attachment, everything that is valuable for him. He is reduced to nothing and when there is nothing left to lose, he sees God. "Now I know you in my flesh." This is a miracle: a contraction of consciousness, losing its identification with everything, then seeing God, experiencing God, followed by a period of expansion when everything becomes real again, as you portrayed in ascending-descending the mountain. You are now fighting to get back into reality and unite the spiritual with the material. Job is a beautiful archetype for letting go of everything, total dis-identification with everything, then finding an amazing moment of connection, expansion, re-identification, freshly reattaching, so that one learns to use one's capacities in a new way. A rhythm of contraction-expansion, like heartbeats, breathing, and other body-emotive pulsing.

Eds: You both speak of body–mind–spirit in language of pulsation, a rhythmical language, sexual even. How does the connection between the three serve your practice?

OE: I work a lot with sensuality, with people who are completely not integrated with parts of themselves, and I feel inspired to do peace-making in some way. Rabbi Nachman of Breslav speaks about people whose parts are at war with each other, not getting along—either physically or spiritually, so I see my work as integration, peace-making between different parts, different countries, or within the individual. We learn to recognise that we are all parts of the same organism and need one another—spiritual parts need carnal parts and vice versa. And we can start to appreciate all those parts and find how they can work together. What you relate to, Mike, as going up and down, in and out, or even—as I see it—masculine and feminine, are polarities. We could perceive ourselves in the middle of these polarities, at their centre. This is a dynamic process, I can spread my arms to all directions and hold my world in peace. This in Kabbalah is called the *Sfira of Tiferet*. The term *Tiferet* comes from the stem of the grape vine, it is the one who stands in the middle of the branches of the vine. *Tiferet* is the trunk of the tree. And any work that helps me hold everything that I am, from the most physical to the spiritual, is a healing work.

ME: It is very lovely, Ohad, and, you know, Freud speaks of times where something has gone wrong with the rhythm of the psyche. Rhythm is a basic musical feeling and experience, allied with timing, the timing of the psyche, the timing of music, timing of experiences, timing of possibilities. For example, in and out are not just sexual, but also characterise breathing. Breathing is potentially healing. Breathing in–out is allied with letting in and letting out emotionally as well. Eating is another of our multiple in–out systems. I like your notion of peace-making, which reminds me of William Blake's image of heaven (1790), where all voices of psyche, spirit, body, soul have their say, a kind of war of viewpoints that are mutually nourishing.

OE: And what is your image, Mike, of healing?

ME: My own particular image is a little more subdued. I talk about becoming better partners with our capacities. We have so many capacities and so many states that our capacities give birth to, how do we partner them in a more amiable way, so that they may all contribute? We have this problem not just with ourselves but throughout the world, states at war with each other. Rabbi Nachman of Breslov was asked why meditation in the forest can be a tormenting experience. He answered that usually we have someone to fight with. We need someone to fight with. If we don't have somebody to fight with we fight with ourselves.

I thought of another experience when you were talking about coming down the mountain. It is the story of Rabbi Shimon bar Yochai going up the mountain with his son to escape the Romans for many years. While they are in the mountains, revelations of the Zohar are given to them in their high spiritual state. When they come down and see actual people and see how flawed everybody is, their eyes start burning up the people. Their eyes see the flaws in everybody, inferior beings who have not reached the high states Rabbi Shimon and his son did, and start burning these people with their looks. And then God says: "Back up the mountain with you, what are you doing?

These are alive people, living souls. You haven't learned what you need to learn yet; so try again."

OE: It's indeed a beautiful story. It ends when two years later they go again down the mountain and the young one, the son, is still burning, yet the father, Rabbi Shimon, is healing every place where his son is burning. It is the more mature consciousness that can be in peace with the world.

ME: Yes, and these are amazing dimensions shared by all groups of people—east and west expressed in myriad ways, as we are doing now. We have all kinds of metaphors expressing experiences rich with possibilities. So much is unknown. What we know is only a spark compared with what we don't know, an important spark with which we do amazing things—talk on telephones, use computers, read books, build the Taj Mahal. I think that between faith and belief, faith is ineffable and deeper and has to do with the unknown. Belief is something we fight over: my experience is right, yours wrong. But if one is rooted in the unknown, as well as the known, we are less likely to be hurtful to one another. If I think I know all about my partner, I lose the mystery of our beings. I've come to feel more and more there is an ethics of the unknown, that the unknown protects us from ourselves, from our aggressive, knowing selves.

OE: I really like the notion of the ethics of the unknown, thank you Mike. I live in Israel and experience it a lot; what we project on the other and think that we know them, what they mean. And indeed an important part of peace-making on all levels begins with experiencing the unknown and stepping back to be in awe of how much we actually don't know, and appreciate the mystery of life. I think this is the core of Martin Buber's (1958) I–thou, the other becomes thou and not an it when I step back and leave space for the unknown. We realise today that cosmology is a mystery; that everything is actually orbiting the mystery since the centre of our galaxy is a black hole. This is a shift in human consciousness. It is admitting the unknown is the centre of our search, and is a step of awe and towards realisation, as well as a joyous sign. And how are you, Mike?

ME: I am a mixture. I have different feelings and sensations in different parts of me, as if my body is a living soul and my soul a living body, with lots of dimensions of experience. My overall feeling is I'm glad to be alive! At my age and condition, to have another day, to talk with people in this mysterious way, people I have never met or seen and may never see. I am grateful that God gave me life for this moment, and also feel a little frustration because I don't know if I was adequate and communicated my ideas clearly enough.

Eds: Thank you both for your enlightening conversation.

PART VII

THE PSYCHOTHERAPIST'S BODY

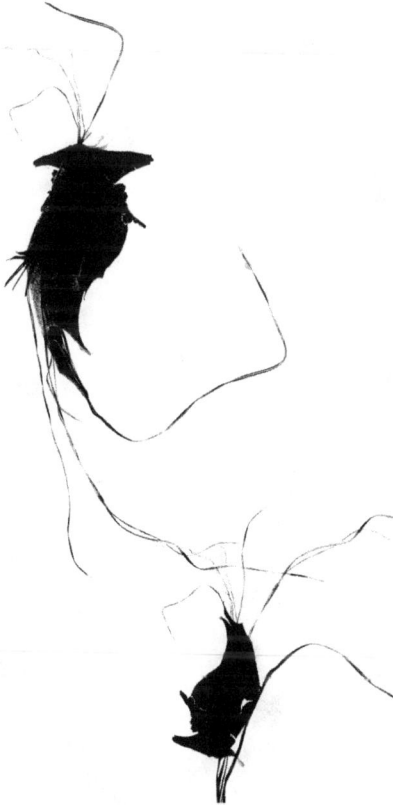

Introduction to Part VII

A s psychotherapists and psychoanalysts, we bring ourselves into a clinical encounter. We attempt to arrive as fully as we can; to really be there. We give ourselves to the person with whom we sit; we give our thoughts, our feelings, our understandings. And our bodies, whether these are given or not, they join us too and are often far more visible than we would have liked.

Freud (1913c) was very sensitive to the psychoanalyst's visibility. He wrote:

> I cannot put up with being stared at by other people for eight hours a day (or more) since, while I am listening to the patient, I, too, give myself over to the current of my unconscious thoughts, I do not wish my expressions of face to give the patient material for interpretations or to influence him in what he tells me. (pp. 133–134)

Today, we realise that while the analyst's impact on the client is inevitable, it is also true vice versa. The analytic and therapeutic encounter is saturated with mutual influence. Frequently, this influence is somatic before it is emotional or cognitive. Our bodies sense the other person's body. The other senses us. A meeting is thus not only meeting of minds, but also—and perhaps more so—meeting of bodies.

Psychoanalyst and somatic psychotherapist John Conger wrote extensively on the place of the body in psychotherapy (e.g., 1988, 1994), and brings the wealth and breadth of his experience to exploring this issue. He is joined by Asaf Rolef Ben-Shahar, who is particularly curious about the benefits and prices of working relationally with the body. Following their individual papers, John and Asaf set to share and discuss issues of embodiment and disembodiment, shame, risk, and disciplined practice. They find a shared language that bridges the generational gap between them.

CHAPTER EIGHTEEN

Responding to a boundary

John Conger

O n 20 December 1969, while visiting her father in North Carolina, at twenty-nine years old, my wife was thrown from a horse and died. My wife gone, I awoke to a dream of my house engulfed in flame. For weeks afterward, I was held in that vision, consumed in flame day after day, my anguish, my regrets, my hopes, my heart, my entire life, all burned to earth by that implacable boundary of death. I had no way to go on, no past, no future, but remarkably, I was still present and self-aware. In its extremity, the vision numbed me, separated me, as if held by a fierce angel. In my despair, I wished for death. I was lifted up for an instant and given a glimpse of a better time.

During the summer of 1970, I left everything. At thirty-five years old with my four-year-old son, at the completion of my teaching job, I drove across the country in my Ford Torino to Berkeley, California. Outside my apartment, there was still, now and again, riot police in orange jumpsuits piling out of buses. I had sold my house in New Jersey; I had left my job; I had abandoned my doctorate program at NYU in English Literature. I got as far away from the pain as I physically could. With the help of a woman friend and a year of stumbling about, I began a doctorate in psychology in San Francisco.

In Berkeley, I decided I could bear no more pain. I stopped running for exercise and in every way I slowed down and withdrew. One day I woke up with a constricting pressure around my chest, just as if I had put on a T-shirt that was too small, a tightness that did not go away. I had just attended a conference on Reich in San Francisco. My analyst did not understand why I might not choose to analyse the constriction away.

I chose instead a Reichian analyst who, within a few sessions, released me from such tension. But the Reichian did not believe in talk at all. Years later in 1978, after being worked on by Rolfers, chiropractors, acupuncturists, masseurs—finally, licensed as a psychologist, I stumbled into a Bioenergetics training. Bioenergetics is a neo-Reichian process developed by Al Lowen, a student of Reich, in which a range of postures, standing and lying down, and the inclusion of verbal and somatic analysis are employed. More recently I became a psychoanalyst, and so in my pretension, I claim to practise a somatic psychoanalysis.

It seems that all our words throw the body into shadow. I believe that before we developed verbal language 120,000 years ago, we were talking up a storm; our body, through gestures and intuition, knew what was communicated. But verbal language, our brilliant new toy in its disembodied freedom, tossed somatic language aside. Suffering such neglect, our bodies still talk to us, but who is listening?

What matters in this psyche-soma work might as easily have happened a thousand years ago by a healer in a tribe along a river. As healers, we must be grounded and present, attentive to the somatic dialogue with the client, and have tools that define and heighten the experience of the body area that concerns us.

When I entered into Bioenergetic analysis with Eleanor Greenlee, an international Bioenergetic trainer, I discovered that my energy was gathered around my head and upper body. Gradually I learned to feel my feet supported by the earth, to challenge and relax the musculature of the legs, to breathe down into my belly, to relax my pelvis, to open up my tight chest with an easy, full breath, to loosen my shoulders, to bring flexibility to a rigid spine, to loosen the tight bands of my neck, to make grotesque faces in the mirror, to check out the gag reflex, to hit and kick and protest, to lie inert on a bed and be comforted with a hand on my back or on my belly, to fall into the rhythm of the orgasm reflex; and ultimately, to feel the pulse of breath create a small energetic wave that related the body to itself and the earth—to be fully, somatically present. In the words of Ram Dass, to *be here now*.

As a trainer, I realised that to be entirely present with another person, I need to ground, have secure boundaries, uninhibited breath, a range of feeling, an intention to be here on the planet (not just as an accident), and an uninhibited energetic flow—what I call The Six Foundations.

The vignette I wish to describe, replete with my countertransference, comes out of my discovery of these principles that define my work. These days I have not forgotten how to be stupid, but no matter how my day unfolds, I can always ground in the presence of my clients and read the energy flowing or trapped in the body. But as it turned out, I learned the most one weekend some years ago, instructing my first training group, by being the fool.

I realised from teaching introductory classes in somatic therapy in graduate school, that when facing off as a demonstration with a student, both of us standing, that as I approached the student, I observed a contradiction. Frequently the student invited me to come closer while his/her body and face reacted in discomfort and fear. At other times, I saw a student's face melt and open, the defences dropping away, revealing a great beauty and vulnerability one sees at times only with a lover. How was I to understand these experiences?

Grounding and being present and connected energetically is the fundamental purpose in Bioenergetic training. In 2003, when I began training a group to be credentialed (typically a four to six year process), I did not realise that my own capacity to ground varied from client to client.

One day with my group, I asked a student to play the therapist and the second student the client, to stand about eight feet apart. Rather than the therapy, my focus was on whether the therapist was able to ground up against the provocative presence of another person as client, a challenge we ordinarily take for granted. The therapist, on the other hand, was in a hurry to do the therapy. "Are you grounded," I asked the student?

"Oh yes, now I am."

"No, actually you are not. Bring your attention down to your feet and legs. Shift your weight this way (I would demonstrate). Breathe up from the earth and down."

Grounding depends on being fully present somatically and intentionally with the client. Soon, I became frustrated with the repeated failure of my students to ground. I chose to demonstrate myself, as the therapist, the "correct way" while providing the class with an intimate blow by blow account of my inner struggle in the face of another person. With my superior attitude, I thought this process would be easy. The first student was easy to ground with and took barely a minute. I felt a trust with him, and my body felt strong and securely placed.

The second client was a woman in her early thirties who often joked with me affectionately like a brother–sister rough-house pushing or pulling. When she stood up about eight feet away, I expected the easy play to ground me immediately, but the opposite was true. She teased me across the distance by acting sexy, just a brief moment, a look and turn of shoulder before she grounded herself with a big smile.

But rather than being easily amused by the game, I was thrown into an ungrounded, shadowy state. I was suddenly a young boy up against a popular, high school girl, face to face suddenly, in the hall. I was reporting and laughing moment by moment, awkwardly to my class about being unable to find my feet, a shrinking, hunched, withdrawing urge, so foolish, so inept, before the unobtainable high school goddess, a surging memory of past disembodied embarrassment, all somatically recalled, after all these years unacknowledged and passed over by a hopeful life of promise. Amid laughter at my candour, I took some time to pull myself together out of my humiliated, adolescent shadow—sufficient time to ground and be present and clear.

In a bold effort to recover, I proceeded. The next student to play my client held another relational energy entirely. She looked up at me in utter respect, gratitude, and vulnerability. Up against her energy, I felt like quite the charismatic master—grounded and powerful, very much the Man, in every way a narcissistic danger to myself and others.

Within a few minutes, my entire sense of an embodied-self shifted. I saw how being present and grounded was an ongoing and uncertain affair, that I had no certainty independent of my client and the particular moment. My work and experience did not render me immune and special. Somatically, every encounter is as if for the first time. My therapy was dramatically and unconditionally relational. The boundary exercise brought home to me that day the uncertain trial of being present, intentional and grounded upon which our therapeutic purposes entirely depend.

With the boundary exercise, I stand about eight feet away from a new client. I approach the client one step at a time and study their response, most particularly the face and eyes where the fear, arousal, concern so immediately show themselves. The client's social training speaks to me saying "come closer, that's fine", but at one of my steps forward, the client's face says "Yikes". I stop. I take a small step back. I ask, "How does this feel?"

I describe what I see and tell their body that I am paying attention to its concern. My body is listening to their body. I have made a proper introduction. Now I suspect with time, my client's body will trust me when I get close or touch. My client's body will whisper to my body and my intuition will lead me to intervene in a useful way. At the same time, I notice how my body feels up against this current stranger. I must be listening and adapting my work to this far earlier communication as a two way street. That attunement is at the heart of somatic analytic therapy.

I think as therapists, it helps to have learned from the disasters that haunt our lives, that we are recovering therapists, not disconnected and immune to the extraordinary pain of so many of our clients. Who can experience life without anguish and humiliation, without some evidence of innocent stupidity, some horror from the buried past in which our sense of self is hopelessly compromised? When we walk this path as therapists out of our own neglect and longing, our own troubled journey in the wilderness of our shadow, we do well to meet our clients with the dignity that comes from self-awareness, with the nakedness of being intentionally, somatically present.

CHAPTER NINETEEN

Like love

Asaf Rolef Ben-Shahar

About being a body

Zohar and I are taking a stroll in a nearby wood; she is almost seven. "It's weird, daddy," she says, "in all the books I'm reading they never speak of eating or drinking, peeing, pooing or being ill. But eating and pooing and peeing and feeling unwell are all part of life." Two days earlier she said: "It seems that everybody likes having a body but I don't want to be a body. I prefer to be a soul without a body. Life is painful."

At sixteen, my school year sets out for a fieldtrip in the southern town of Eilat. The tents are set and most kids are excited. I feel ambivalent. I always feel ambivalent in crowds, easily lost, ill at ease. Dusk is approaching and everybody is in a hurry to set the camp. To my horror I discover that people are beginning to disappear. First, their feet fade away. I rub my eyes to make sure I am not hallucinating; I am not. Feetless people float around the campsite. As time goes by more and more of their bodies disappear: the calves and shins, the knees, the thighs, and pelvises. Heads are afloat, and I check my own hands, my own body, to make sure it is still here. Am I going crazy? Nothing exists from the necks down, as if the Nothing from *The Never-Ending*

Story has taken over. I tell nobody, but dread spreads all over me as thoroughly as the darkness spreads over the mountains of Eilat.

It took three more years to diagnose my problem as a form of night blindness, a difficulty in adapting to changes in light and to properly see during certain hours. At the beginning, nobody believed me. During my military induction I nearly died and killed a few friends. My commander instructed a friend to hold my hand at night. I was lead to the toilet, from the showers to the guarding position. I remember his dry hand holding mine and my hand reaching out to feel him, relying on him as my eyes. I felt shame.

As Zohar and I are walking in the wood we can hear the calling of a kingfisher; a brisk succession of sharp and high-pitched calls. The kingfisher goes hunting.

Shame; that was the first feeling I had about my body. Not necessarily about anything specific about my body, but more about having to have a body: about being a body. The necessity to eat, the continuous body pain, the difficulty in being a body among other bodies— these were always hard to bear. I thought that most people found it easier to have bodies, to be bodies. It was only when I discovered sex that being a body became a thing of joy and celebration and not just shame and suffering. To this date, sex is perhaps the only shame-free area of my life. Engaging with all things concerning the intimate meeting of bodies, it is only there that my body can rest. Would my daughter Zohar have to wait that long?

Always in pain

"Turn off the light please."

"Can we just sit without talking."

"Can you hold me; tight, but not too tight."

"I always hurt," she said and I believed her. "It never feels good to be in me." She was twenty seven, petit and pretty, intelligent and functional; "unless of course I smoke weed or drink." She came to see me for body-psychotherapy, with the remote hope of easing some of her physical pain, which accompanied her fibromyalgia. Could she be persuaded that it was actually good to have a body, to be a body? By the time I met her I was deeply converted into the religion of psychotherapy in general, and specifically body-psychotherapy, believing in the beauty and joy of having a body, of embodying our pleasures and pains. I have learned to enjoy food, to enjoy sleeping and other physical activities (even sports, which I used to hate). We sat in the dark and I held her. Our breathing slowly synchronised and I could not see anything. "Are you in pain right now?" I asked, arrogantly (or naively) hoping that my therapeutic intervention introduced a change. "I am," she said, "I always hurt. It never feels good to be in me." Her name was Frances.

I was twenty-eight when we met, and we worked for six years together. It was hard work. At first I worked very hard and Frances obliged me, like a parent reluctantly following her hyperactive child in the playground. With great enthusiasm I attempted to introduce joyous bodily experiences to Frances, and although she really did enjoy bodywork, and responded well to myriad of trauma-work techniques, it always felt that Frances obliged passively. She was not there.

We spent many sessions in complete darkness with an alarm clock to indicate the endings of our sessions. Her hand would reach out to hold mine in the dark, patiently waiting to be met. Her hand was dry and cold, like the hand of my friend in the army. Only this time she was the one seeking out and I was there to guide, or so I thought. Our connection was comforting for us both, but it did not alleviate pain. "How much would you charge for taking all the pain and suffering instead of me?" she jokingly asked one day and I realised it was exactly what I was trying to do, and kept failing at that.

Frances tried killing herself once, at sixteen. Her fibromyalgia began at nineteen. The physical pain replaced an even more unbearable psychic pain of abuse and betrayal, from the closest people to her. Her mother was so devastated with Frances' suicide attempt that she too tried killing herself shortly afterwards and Frances immediately abandoned her own suffering and attended to her mother. "Everybody is working really hard to eradicate suffering," my supervisor said, "what an honourable and futile effort." It made me very angry, "What do you expect me to do?" I furiously asked her, "give up?" She shook her head, "Just be there with your own body."

Just being there

"I'm having an attack," Frances says.

"Hold my hand."

"Please don't try to make it better."

"Just be with me."

Maternal countertransference was obvious, but it did not end there. In my own life I had fought to transform my body of shame into an embodied celebration. By the white of my knuckles I held on to this positive, life-affirming approach to body.

Sitting with Frances, I breathed, and it hurt. It was so dark and it was getting claustrophobic for me. My hand was sweaty.

I am at a military base underground. It is pitch-black and the soldiers are expected to learn their way by heart. I cannot breathe. My forehead is bleeding since I keep banging my head against the tunnel's walls, which I fail to notice. I wait for someone to come so that I may hold their hand and get to the living quarters. Somebody approaches. Full of shame I ask him, "Can I hold your hand, please? I cannot see anything." The guy, whom I do not know, takes my sweaty cold hand, "you're sweating" he says, "I don't like it; just hold on to my shirt."

It feels that the temperature in the clinic has suddenly dropped. "Is it me or did it really get cold in here?" I ask Frances. "It's you, Asaf," she responds.

We sit together for what must have been twenty minutes or so but feels like eternity. My body is shaking with pain, with fear, with anger, and with cold. Some of it is mine, surely some resonate Frances'? Her body too is shaking. Her hand is dry and mine is sweaty. Who is holding whom? In the darkness I can hear her breathing change and she starts crying; quietly first, then louder. I am surprised to discover that my own cheeks are getting wet. I must be crying too. No words are spoken, no interpretations made. Momentarily, our hands let go of one another and my hand reaches out for her face, touching her wet cheeks. Frances does the same and she can feel my own tears.

"I really don't like being a body right now," I say.

"I know, Asaf, that's why I came to see you. You know what it's like."

Ambivalent bodies

Bodies speak of pain and joy. They speak of our own history and that of our parents and their parents in turn. My young daughters are already facing the complicated task of embodying, of the first noble truth, "there is suffering in the world." Bodies also reflect bodies around them. There is no such thing as a body, suggested Susie Orbach (2003): "There is only a body in relationship with another body" (p. 10).

And clients step into the clinic and sit their hurting bodies on the chair or couch or mattress. And their hurt reverberates in my psyche, which might be worked through in supervision. But their pains also awaken my bodily pain, concrete pain. Concrete fears are embodied in the clinic, cold sweat and tearful eyes, dry skin and breathlessness, contracted muscles and startle reflexes.

"It hurts being in this reality," Zohar says, "it has so many unpleasant bodily things."

I was attracted to the field of body psychotherapy because of my ambivalence towards being a body. Secretly, I hoped that training and therapy would help me overcome the pain of having a body, of being a body. I entered this profession with a disowned desire to rid myself of my somatic presence. In holding on to Eros and its sublimated therapeutic forms I sought to eradicate Thanatos, within whose embrace I once spent many years. My body haunted me, though, and still does, claiming its multifaceted reality. The attempts to focus only on the vital, excited, and life-seeking aspects of my body often resulted in my client's holding the shadow of the body in my stead, on behalf of our dyad. Time and again, I am called to open myself and feel the river of embodied life flowing within me and between me and the other: good and bad, painful and joyous, erotic and deadening. And when I manage to surrender the body's call, something novel stands a chance of unfolding.

"It is a very remarkable thing that the unconscious can react upon another, without passing through consciousness," wrote Freud (1915e, p. 194), and I believe that what he described was primarily a bodily phenomenon—resonance. I see resonance as the socio-biological foundation for transference and projective identification. Our bodies are the first to respond to another person since we are, as Freud (1923b) wisely noted, first and foremost of the body. Be it consciously or unconsciously, all psychotherapists practise bodily attunement to their clients as a way of responding and recognising the whereabouts of the other. Body psychotherapists do so with greater attention to somatic processes—both their own and those of their clients (Levy, 2013; Oschman, 2000; Rolef Ben-Shahar, 2008, 2014).

As we continue our walk we enter a graveyard. Some of the trees are very old, and Shuy Grace, my three-year-old, takes her sandals off and runs to touch its bark and chase a squirrel. "I like it here," I say, "it is ever so peaceful." Zohar looks at me solemnly, "it's because they don't have bodies anymore, so it doesn't hurt them. But I don't want to die, because this life has also some pleasurable and connecting things as well and I need a body for that." Zohar pauses and looks at me and I am full of awe with her. Her dramatic expression also makes me smile. After a thematic pause my daughter takes my hand and looks straight ahead at an old grave as she says: "like love, for example."

Shuy Grace holds my other hand, "I'll protect you from the dark," she announces, "and you'll protect me from monsters." I think this is a fair deal.

CHAPTER TWENTY

Dialogue: falling off the horse

John Conger and Asaf Rolef Ben-Shahar

A saf Rolef Ben-Shahar: I was quite thrown off by the similarities of our approaches in our pieces.

John Conger: I too was struck by a couple of powerful similarities, one was humiliation.

AR: You said humiliation was your middle name.

JC: I was thinking of your daughter's saying "I don't want to be in a body". I too approach the body from a sense of not having a sense of self. I didn't have a sense of self, so it was through the body that I was desperately searching for a sense or location of a self.

AR: What you speak of is getting a sense of self through the body. I'm thinking of "the psyche indwelling in the soma" (Winnicott, 1988, p. 44). This is, ideally, a gradual process. But for both you and I, and in both of our written pieces here, the self was not a given; it had to be earned. We both made desperate attempts to have a body, with the shadow of the body rather than the light of the body as the primary entrance portal.

JC: Yes. And there is one sentence I wanted to ask you about that was a model sentence, "As Zohar and I are walking in the woods we can

161

hear the calling of a kingfisher; a brisk succession of sharp and high-pitched calls. The kingfisher goes hunting."

AR: Some people are granted their body, and they don't have to gain their body. I feel that both of us had to claim our bodies and ourselves through being bodies. There is a paradox herein: a kingfisher whose voice and being is naturally embodied, walking with a seven-year-old who is so complex; perhaps we can only survive this complexity when it resides alongside a truly simple existence that includes the body as well. And this relates for me to the beginning of your piece about your wife being thrown off the horse. You too, we too are thrown of the horse time and again, with every client. How can we trust to survive this fall?

JC: Just like the woman with fibromyalgia you describe, who needed you to be with her, not help her by doing. And that's about soul, not body. The healing there did not come from therapy, but rather from the soul, from being completely present with somebody, which is the centre piece of our work. I once worked with a very borderline and brilliant woman. Our work practically killed me for four years. She invaded my lifestyle, oblivious to my attempts to put up a firewall and to all my efforts to heal her. Yet she was the one who could reach down into my own borderline areas, scratching it and opening me up. She was the only person and the only client I have ever screamed at. And I knew I could.

When I worked with her it nearly killed me and people asked me why do you do that? And I'm grateful to her because I never got to that place in myself before. And your client did the same for you.

AR: In a way you say that both my client and yours were refusing to satisfy our narcissistic needs to be good therapists. They wouldn't provide . . . I tried really hard, I was making efforts, and she wouldn't provide. In effect, she said if you want to work with me you have to fall off the horse. And right this moment I don't understand, why do we do that? And how can we trust that we would neither lose our sanity nor die?

JC: I tend to say these days that if I stretch my arms up parallel in front of me that's about the amount that I can take in, but when I stretch my arms up in either direction that's how big our experience is. Jung defined the self, not just in terms of who we are but also of what we are becoming, so the whole idea of sorrow changes, freeing me to consider a higher ethics—of developing. When I stop thinking in terms of client and begin to think about healing, then the ongoing negotiation of boundaries change. Boundaries are important, they are not just abstract rules, but sometimes there are clients that take us to dissolve these in order for the healing to take place—allowing ourselves to be touched in places we couldn't otherwise reach. Like your client, who you could hold and be with her isolation since you have been so isolated yourself.

AR: But I think it's more than that John, it's not only that I have known her isolation because I have been there, but moreover that she held me at that time as well.

JC: Exactly!

AR: And you are right in saying that we have little certainty independent of our clients, and it's really scary, so the boundaries of not working directly with bodies also protect us from the reality that bodies are always relational; that even if the client cannot interpret what we show them, we are showing them our shame, our humiliation, our guilt, our fears, and they are attuned to that; even if you are a psychoanalyst sitting behind your clients they sense you up.

JC: That's right, they know, the body knows.

AR: I'm wondering what it means if we are so exposed to our clients, because some of them come with quite disturbed stories, and we are there, naked. How do you deal with the price of it?

JC: You are right, but that's also our gift. The way I understand it, when verbal language was developed our body was already taking up a storm, and that's where the seeds of consciousness and feeling stem from. And in the development of verbal language we split off into the body shadow, but our nakedness concerns letting go of the social mask and being present in the language of the body, where the images of our client's body communicate with the unspoken parts of our body.[1] When I can put aside my social veneer and feel vulnerable, my body is present with this client's body and I can be attuned to myself and the other.

AR: I feel the same thing, when therapy works then we have sex. It might not be penetrative sex but we pulsate between symbiosis and separation. There is a real penetration of both our psyches and soul, and my clients enter me just as much as I do them, and I'm wondering . . . aren't we also risking sexually transmitted diseases?

JC: Psychological sexually transmitted disease.

AR: Yes!

JC: I'm seventy-nine today. When I was in my forties, and a young woman in her twenties came to therapy, I would sometimes not work with her, because I felt I wouldn't manage it, because at that time my sense of loving was very sexual.

AR: So if you could, with all these years of experience, offer supervision to this younger John would you still tell him not to work with her?

JC: No, I would tell him to go ahead; there was an edge for him to meet. But in our culture and in this country I had to develop a very careful way of working in the body.[2] In Berkley every other person is either a therapist or a lawyer, and we think twice of what we say or think. It is a puritan culture and I need to be very precise because I don't want to lose my license.

AR: John, you said that in order to be present you "need to ground, to have secure boundaries, uninhibited breath, a range of feelings, an intention to be here on the planet, and an uninhibited energetic flow". And I thought, I can probably do it ten per cent of the time if I'm lucky, and what happens when I'm not? If I had a fight with my partner or if my daughters gave me a hard time, or when I'm having a bad day . . . How do we manage our imperfections?

JC: I think that you can have a sense of your own un-groundedness which is a way of taking responsibility. But there are ways in which if we don't pay attention to our un-groundedness we are really in trouble. For me a lot of it is very physical, I have to feel my feet on the ground and feel the energetic flow into my pelvis and then begin to see, recognise that right this moment my body is a little split and then I look at the person and think: am I present here?

AR: So it's about minding our body.

JC: Yes, and about taking the time to process how I feel before I jump in the water. Because once I jump in the water then I'm in a state of hysteria. If I can feel myself grounded before I jump, if I can realise that there is a client there in the distance—that is safe enough. I am then able to sense that I am present in my body now and sense the client's body now; not just running on social grace, that I'm actually there with my body feeling their body and the impact they have on me. In the grounding exercise I described in my paper, I was vulnerable to one student and then to the other—in a very different way; and by experiencing it and processing it over and over again, my body learns to talk with their body, and their body talks to me.

AR: I like your dialectics. For me body–psychotherapy has always been frightening because many people were attracted to it because they were so connected to their body and less connected to ideas, and I always felt a little bit like a fraud, because I came into this field because I wanted to have a body not because I had one. And today even in the analytic field there is recognition in the importance of working with body, and I am wondering about the times where it's valuable to not have a body, to celebrate the death of the body, or to at least allow the death of the body, both the body of the client and our own.

JC: This is possibly the time to speak about soul. Your client demanded you gave up your ambition and remained present with her, and the healing nature of these moments is about soul. You were demonstrating to her that you believed in a presence that was outside of the body, that endures, that is separate from the body but present in the body. She needed that reflection, and you held that mirror.

AR: I'm thinking of Steven Mitchell's (2005) saying that if the client doesn't get under your skin then therapy is limited in scope. Can we work with people who bore us? Maybe we need to find something that interests us; something to learn from and to grow from, otherwise . . . when nothing is stirred up no novelty can take place. But isn't it tiring for you to be stirred up time and again?

JC: No, because it's about love. Just like your daughter realised, it's about love. It offers me a practice, a spiritual practice, that's my first and major goal. Being present here-and-now with another person is my practice. And for me, it's so much better than being a monk.

AR: And therapy is only one way of doing it. It makes me think of the difference between having a body and being a body in psychotherapy (see Totton, 2010), and about these outside of therapy.

JC: I see so many clients, and I am alive. Yet when you get past seventy, it's a complex scene. On some levels, it is as if my body is many years younger, and my energy is younger and yet I am not.

AR: You are describing the gap between the vitality and aliveness of your professional body and how much of it is translatable into your personal life, and possibly one of the differences between our papers is the place of sexuality and I guess part of it stage related.

JC: I have actually more recently begun to feel my sexual energy sort of rejuvenating . . . I haven't given up yet.

AR: I wish to speak of something that I haven't seen written, connected to our conversation. I understand and know that we should not have sex with our clients. The taboo is crucial, yet I have never seen, nor have I heard, colleagues discussing the pain of not being able to have sex with clients, and the yearning for the ultimate merge sort of speak.

JC: That would be an important paper to write, and the idea of spiritual and sexual merge which allows us access ourselves to that degree is one of the reasons I was moved by your paper.

AR: For me, this is one of the sad things that we have lost with Freud because in his separating from spirituality, sexuality became only a shadow of the relational and spiritual meeting it can offer.

JC: If we look at Breuer and Anna O. I am certain Breuer didn't molest Anna O, but I think he probably fell in love with her and she was in her early twenties? And he saw her practically every day, and they deepened their relationship and he sensed that experience in the deepest possible way.

AR: So her fantasy of being pregnant was not merely about sexual contact, it was also about the yearning for union and spiritual connection.

JC: He was a doctor, and he went into her bedroom and sat by her bed and the contact must have been very intense.

AR: And you know, John, if I'm thinking of this age, and of bodies, and Skype sessions, and telephone sessions, and it has a lot of disadvantages but I'm also thinking of the power it might have. Because my body has a lot of energy and my bodily presence can also be threatening, and my body impacts . . . the way I look impacts, the way I breathe impacts. Skype sessions and telephone sessions can recreate the idea of the analytic couch.

JC: I had a client years ago, and he lived across the bay, and for a while he couldn't come to see me and we had phone sessions. And he said more on phone than he ever did in person. There is something about talking on the phone . . .

AR: And about not having a body, not having our bodies shoved in our faces. The psychoanalytic couch was also a way of minimising having a body, and I think it's really good to sometimes not have a body if we have choice about that.

JC: I have written a paper to *Contemporary Psychoanalysis* (not yet published), about the contrast between our body-oriented past world, and what I call the cyber-soul, the cyber-body, because now people are living in a cyber-world,

AR: It's a way of having alter-egos or alter-bodies very alive, but our real bodies are beginning to whither. In that respect as body psychotherapists we deliver a strong message both about the pain and the joy of having a body and being a body. I had numerous clients who never had sex without being drunk even with their partner, with their wives with their husbands . . . who never danced without being drunk. They had to work really hard to not have a body before they can engage bodily. It's not easy being bodies. We are thrown off horses all the time.

JC: What drove me to the work itself was this huge crisis of death and the loss of everything, and then the reaction of my body finally got my attention. And my analyst could not understand why I didn't want to analyse my body away . . .

AR: It makes me think of dancing. I love dancing, and I move my body well, as long as nobody tells me what to do, then I get so shame-bound that I freeze. And I noted that what liberated you from technique was using technique at the service of the soul.

JC: The work is not dependent on technique, but on the connection.

AR: This is why I find the reliance on neuroscience, both in psychoanalysis and body psychotherapy, a bit annoying. It makes us prone to change our practices into religion. Techniques are like that, and it doesn't matter if they are psychoanalytic or somatic. And then we need to unpick the technique, like you have done with your student. So what was it like for her to realise her impact on you?

JC: She really knew it to start with. The surprise was not hers but my own. As a trainee, she dared to be seductive with me like nobody else did, and she knew how to play me.

AR: It makes me think of Jonathan Slavin (2013), who wrote a paper about Jody Messler-Davies's "Love in the Afternoon" (1994). Messler-Davies shared an erotic dream she had about a client with that client, and Slavin argues that what she did was not self-disclosure, but a moment of truth, because both of them knew what was happening there, and she simply affirmed that which they both knew. So, your client served you with an embodied moment of truth.

JC: Exactly. And as a somatic psychoanalyst, I have adopted many tools and interdisciplinary skills for allowing those moments of truth to occur, I am less bound to one method. The fact that I did somatic work is intriguing to people and people come to me and the way in is not as interesting as the encounter.

AR: But are we as therapists and analysts flexible enough to allow our religion to include other material? Can we allow ourselves to be ungrounded as a profession to enable novelty, to fall off the horse as a bigger body?

JC: In my pursuit for growth, I have gone after my own healing and the love affair I had was the meeting with clients, and these relationships healed me as they healed you. We seek our own healing, and I also found that the body holds material that is often inaccessible by verbal interaction alone. And I am grateful for my experience, both professionally and for me.

AR: Thank you. It is a privilege both to speak with you and to sense that I'm not alone.

JC: Thank you. It's like finding a soulmate across the sea.

Notes

1. Very similar to Freud's conceptualisation of unconscious-to-unconscious conversation in "The uncanny" (1919h).
2. See Sue Shapiro's (1996) excellent paper on the embodied analyst in the consulting room and Rolef Ben-Shahar's (2007) paper on accountability, as well as Sandra Blooms's excellent series of papers "Neither liberty nor safety" (2004–2006). [Editors]

REFERENCES

Aron, L., & Starr, K. (2013). *A Psychotherapy for the People: Towards a Progressive Psychoanalysis*. Hove: Routledge.

Asheri, S. (2004). Erotic desire in the therapy room. Dare we embody it? Can we afford not to? Paper presented at the 2004 UKCP Conference, London. Retrieved from http://www.yobeely.f2s.com/articles/erotic desire.html

Atwood, M. (1985). *The Handmaid's Tale*. Toronto: McClelland & Stewart.

Balaskas, J. (1983). *Active Birth*. London: Unwin.

Balint, M. (1968). *The Basic Fault. Therapeutic Aspects of Regression*. London: Tavistock.

Bateson, G. (1979). *Mind and Nature: A Necessary Unity*. Cresskill, NJ: Hampton, 2002.

Beebe, B., Knoblauch, S. H., Rustin, J., & Sorter, D. (2005). *Forms of Intersubjectivity in Infant Research and Adult Treatment*. New York: Other Press.

Benjamin, J. (1988). *The Bonds of Love: Psychoanalysis, Feminism, and the Problem of Domination*. New York: Pantheon.

Benjamin, J. (1990). Recognition and destruction: an outline of intersubjectivity. In: S. A. Mitchell & L. Aron (Eds.), *Relational Psychoanalysis: The Emergence of a Tradition* (pp. 181–210). New York: Analytic Press, 1999.

Benjamin, J. (2007). Intersubjectivity, Thirdness, and Mutual Recognition— A talk given at the Institute for Contemporary Psychoanalysis, Los Angeles, CA. Retrieved from http://icpla.edu/wp-content/uploads/2013/03/Benjamin-J.-2007-ICP-Presentation-Thirdness-present-send.pdf on 24 March 2015.

Bion, W. R. (1994). *Cogitations*. In: F. Bion (Ed.). London: Karnac.

Blake, W. (1790). The Marriage of Heaven and Hell. In: M. Mason (Ed.), *William Blake: Selected Poetry*. New York: Oxford University Press.

Bloom, S. L. (2004a). Neither liberty nor safety: the impact of fear on individuals, institutions, and society, part I. *Psychotherapy and Politics International*, 2(2): 78–98.

Bloom, S. L. (2004b). Neither liberty nor safety: the impact of fear on individuals, institutions, and society, part II. *Psychotherapy and Politics International*, 2(3): 212–228.

Bloom, S. L. (2005). Neither liberty nor safety: the impact of fear on individuals, institutions, and society, part III. *Psychotherapy and Politics International*, 3(2): 96–111.

Bloom, S. L. (2006). Neither liberty nor safety: the impact of fear on individuals, institutions, and society, part IV. *Psychotherapy and Politics International*, 4(1): 4–23.

Boadella, D. (1982). Transference, resonance and interference. *Journal of Biodynamic Psychology*, 3: 73–93.

Boadella, D., & Specht Boadella, S. (2006). Basic Concepts in Biosynthesis. *The USA Body Psychotherapy Journal*, 5(1): 18–20.

BODI Group Members, The (2015). The acquisition of a body: establishing a new paradigm and introducing a clinical tool to explore the intergenerational transmission of embodiment. In: J. Petrucelli (Ed.), *Body-States: Interpersonal and Relational Perspectives on the Treatment of Eating Disorders*. New York: Routledge.

Buber, M. (1958). *I and Thou*, R. G. Smith (Trans.). New York: Scribner.

Bucci, W. (1997). *Psychoanalysis and Cognitive Science: A Multiple Code Theory*. New York: Guilford Press.

Butler, J. (1990). *Gender Trouble: Feminism and the Subversion of Identity*. New York: Routledge.

Capra, F. (1982). *The Turning Point*. London: Flamingo.

Capra, F. (2002). *The Hidden Connections*. London: Flamingo.

Chodorow, N. J. (2012). Analytic listening and the five senses: introduction. *Journal of the American Psychoanalytic Association*, 60: 747–758.

Conger, J. P. (1988). *Jung & Reich: the Body as Shadow*. Berkeley, CA: North Atlantic, 2005.

Conger, J. P. (1994). *The Body in Recovery: Somatic Psychotherapy and the Self.* Berkeley, CA: Frog.

Connelly, D. M. (1994). *Traditional Acupuncture: The Law of the Five Elements* (2nd edn). Columbia, SC: Traditional Acupuncture Institute.

Cornell, W. F. (2008). Self in action. In: F. S. Anderson (Ed.), *Bodies in Treatment – The Unspoken Dimension* (pp. 29–49). Hove: Analytic Press.

Descartes, R. (1641). Meditations on first philosophy. In: M. D. Wilson (Ed.), *The Essential Descartes*. New York: Meridian, 1983.

Eigen, M. (2006). *Lust*. Middletown, CT: Wesleyan University Press.

Eigen, M. (2007). *Feeling Matters*. London: Karnac.

Eigen, M. (2012). *Kabbalah and Psychoanalysis*. London: Karnac.

Eigen, M. (2014a). *A Felt Sense: More Explorations of Psychoanalysis and Kabbalah*. London: Karnac.

Eigen, M. (2014b). *The Birth of Experience*. London: Karnac.

Freud, S. (1913c). On beginning the treatment (Further recommendations on the technique of psycho-analysis I). *S.E.*, *12*: 121–144. London: Hogarth.

Freud, S. (1915e). The unconscious. *S. E.*, *14*: 159–215. London: Hogarth.

Freud, S. (1919h). The 'uncanny'. In J. Strachey (Ed.), *S.E.*, *17*: 217–256. London: Hogarth.

Freud, S. (1923b). *The Ego and the Id*. *S. E.*, *19*: 12–66. London: Hogarth.

Goodman, N. (1978). *Ways of Worldmaking*. Indianapolis, IN: Hassocks.

Heinrich-Clauer, V. (2011). Therapists as a resonance body. Which strings come into action? In: V. Heinrich-Clauer, (Ed.), *Handbook—Bioenergetic Analysis*. (pp. 159–177). Gießen: Psycosozial-Verlag.

Huxley, A. (1932). *Brave New World*. London: Flamingo, 1994.

Kalamish Shapira, K. (1961). *Hachsharat Ha'Avrechim*. Tel-Aviv: Zohar.

Kashi-Kark, A. (2011). Knowing pain: the effects of body psychotherapy treatment on a person dealing with chronic pain. *Diploma in Body Psychotherapy thesis*, Reidman College, Tel Aviv.

Knoblauch, S. H. (1997). Beyond the word in psychoanalysis the unspoken dialogue. *Psychoanalytic Dialogues*, *7*(4): 491–516.

Knoblauch, S. H. (1999). The third, minding and affecting: commentary on paper by Lewis Aron. *Psychoanalytic Dialogues*, *9*(1): 41–51.

Knoblauch, S. H. (2000). *The Musical Edge of Therapeutic Dialogue*. Hillsdale, NJ: Analytic Press.

Knoblauch, S. H. (2005). Body rhythms and the unconscious: toward an expanding of clinical attention. *Psychoanalytic Dialogues, 15*(6): 807–827.

Knoblauch, S. H. (2011). Contextualizing attunement within the poly-rhythmic weave: the psychoanalytic samba. *Psychoanalytic Dialogues, 21*(4): 414–427.

Knoblauch, S. H. (2012). Body rhythms and the unconscious: expanding clinical attention with the polyrhythmic wave. In: L. Aron & A. Harris (Eds.), *Relational Psychoanalysis Vol. 5: Evolution of Process* (pp. 183–204). Hove: Routledge.

Lev, A. I., & Malpas, J. (2011). Exploring gender and sexuality in couples and families. At the Edge: Exploring Gender and Sexuality in Couples and Families, *AFTA Monograph Series, 7*: 2–8.

Levy, R. (2013). Relational body psychotherapy as a transpersonal encounter: mutual surrender. *Hebrew Psychology*. Retrieved 19 October 2013 from www.hebpsy.net/articles.asp?t=0&id=3002.

Lipkies, L. (2012). The language of crying in body psychotherapy. *Diploma in Body Psychotherapy*. Reidman College, Tel Aviv.

Looker, T. (1998). "Mama, why don't your feet touch the ground?": staying with the body and the healing moment in psychoanalysis. In: L. Aron & F. S. Anderson (Eds), *Relational Perspectives on the Body* (pp. 237–262). London: Routledge.

Lowen, A. (1965). *Love and Orgasm*. New York: Signet.

Meital, O., & Stav, S. (Eds.) (2013). *Pain in the Flesh: Representations of the Body in Sickness, Suffering, and Jouissance*. Israel: Ben Gurion University and Kinnert: Zmora-Bitan, Dvir Press.

Meltzer, D., & Williams, M. H. (1988). *The Apprehension of Beauty: The Role of Aesthetic Conflict in Development, Art and Violence*. Strath Tay: Clunie.

Merleau-Ponty, M. (1962). *The Primacy of Perception*. Evanston, IL: Northwestern University Press.

Messler-Davies, J. (1994). Love in the afternoon: a relational reconsideration of desire and dread in the countertransference. *Psychoanalytic Dialogues, 4*: 153–170.

Mitchell, S. A. (2000). *Relationality: From Attachment to Intersubjectivity*. Hillsdale, NJ: Analytic Press.

Mitchell, S. A. (2005). *Influence and Autonomy in Psychoanalysis*. Hillsdale, NJ: Analytic Press.

Morin, J. (1995). *The Erotic Mind*. New York: HarperCollins.

Orbach, S. (2003). The John Bowlby Memorial Lecture: the body in clinical practice. Part I: there is no such thing as a body. *British Journal of Psychotherapy, 20*(1): 3–16.

Orbach, S. (2004). What can we learn from the therapist's body? *Attachment & Human Development, 6*(2): 141–150.

Orbach, S. (2009). *Bodies*. London: Profile.

Oschman, J. L. (2000). *Energy Medicine: The Scientific Basis*. Edinburgh: Churchill Livingstone.

Perel, E. (2007). *Mating in Captivity: Sex, Lies and Domestic Bliss*. London: Hodder.

Perel, E. (2010). The double flame: reconciling intimacy and sexuality, retrieving desire. In: S. R. Leiblum, (Ed.), *Treating Sexual Desire Disorders: A Clinical Casebook* (pp. 23–43). New York: Guilford.

Proust, M. (2002). *In Search of Lost Time, Volume 5: The Prisoner and The Fugitive*, C. Clark (Trans.). London: Penguin (first published as *La Prisonnière*, 1923).

Rolef Ben-Shahar, A. (2007). Connecting in the age of accountability. *Self & Society, A Journal of Humanistic Psychology in Britain, 34*(4): 33–38.

Rolef Ben-Shahar, A. (2008). Resonance: the gift of connection. *Self & Society, A Journal of Humanistic Psychology in Britain, 36*(1): 45–48.

Rolef Ben-Shahar, A. (2010). Blanche Wittman's breasts. *Psychotherapy and Politics International, 8*(3): 213–226.

Rolef Ben-Shahar, A. (2013). The self-healing forest: between self-regulation and dyadic regulation. *Body, Movement and Dance in Psychotherapy, 9*(1): 16–28.

Rolef Ben-Shahar. A. (2014). *Touching the Relational Edge: Body Psychotherapy*. London: Karnac.

Rolef Ben-Shahar, A. (2015). Forever young: consumerism and the body of politics from a body psychotherapy perspective. *Psychotherapy and Politics International, 13*(1): 14–29.

Scarry, E. (1985). *The Body in Pain: The Making and Unmaking of the World*. New York: Oxford University Press.

Shapiro, S. A. (1996). The embodied analyst in the Victorian consulting room. *Gender and Psychoanalysis, 1*: 297–322.

Slavin, J. H. (2013). Moments of truth and perverse scenarios in psychoanalysis: revisiting Davies' "Love in the afternoon". *Psychoanalytic Dialogues, 23*(2): 139–149.

Spielrein, S. (1912). Destruction as a cause of coming into being. *Journal of Analytical Psychology, 39*: 155–186, 1994.

Stern, D. N. (1985). *The Interpersonal World of the Infant: A View from Psychoanalysis and Developmental Psychology*. New York: Basic Books.

Stern, D. N. (2004). *The Present Moment in Psychotherapy and Everyday Life*. New York: Norton.

Stern, D. N. (2010). *Forms of Vitality: Exploring Dynamic Experience in Psychology, the Arts, Psychotherapy, and Development*. New York: Oxford University Press.

Stoller, J. (1976). Primary femininity. *Journal of American Psychoanalytic Association, 24*: 54–78.

Strother, E., Lemberg, R., Standord, S. C., & Turbeville, D. (2012). Eating disorders in men: underdiagnosed, undertreated, and misunderstood. *Eating Disorders, 20*(5): 346–355.

Suzuki, S. (2005). *Zen Mind, Beginner's Mind: Informal Talks on Zen Meditation and Practice*. Boston, MA: Shambhala.

Sweetnam, A. (2007). "Are you a woman—or a flower?": the capacity to experience beauty. *The International Journal of Psychoanalysis, 88*(6): 1491–1506.

Symington, N. (1983). The analyst's act of freedom as agent of therapeutic change. *International Review of Psychoanalysis, 10*: 283–291.

Tompkins, P., & Bird, C. (1989). *The Secret Life of Plants*. New York: Harper Collins.

Totton, N. (2005). Embodied relational therapy. In: N. Totton (Ed.), *New Dimensions in Body Psychotherapy* (pp. 168–181). Maidenhead: Open University Press.

Totton, N. (2010). Being, having, and becoming bodies. *Body, Movement and Dance in Psychotherapy, 5*(1): 21–30.

Trevarthen, C. (1998). The concept and foundations of infant intersubjectivity. In: S. Braten (Ed.), *Intersubjective Communication and Emotion in Early Ontogen*. Cambridge: Cambridge University Press.

Trevarthen, C. (2009). The intersubjective psychobiology of human meaning: learning of culture depends on interest for co-operative practical work—and affection for the joyful art of good company. *Psychoanalytic Dialogues, 19*(5): 507–518.

Trevarthen, C., & Aitken, K. J. (2001). Infant intersubjectivity: research, theory, and clinical applications. *Journal of Child Psychology and Psychiatry, 42*(1): 3–48.

Winnicott, D. W. (1971). *Playing and Reality*. London: Routledge.

Winnicott, D. W. (1988). *Human Nature*. New York: Schochen.

Withers, R. (2008). Descartes' dreams. *Journal of Analytical Psychology, 53*: 691–709.

Wolf, N. (1990). *The Beauty Myth*. Toronto: Random House.

Yarom, N. (2013). *Body Dialects: Illuminating Mental Phenomena as Expressed in the Body* (Hebrew edn). Haifa: Pardes.

INDEX

For Product Safety Concerns and Information please contact our EU
representative GPSR@taylorandfrancis.com
Taylor & Francis Verlag GmbH, Kaufingerstraße 24, 80331 München, Germany

www.ingramcontent.com/pod-product-compliance
Lightning Source LLC
Chambersburg PA
CBHW070331270326
41926CB00017B/3841

9 781782 202042